Angela — Be inspired — God is big.
Ann Makena.

KNOWING AND YIELDING TO THE VOICE THAT COUNTS

Help for Facing Life with Faith and Courage

ANN B. MAKENA

WESTBOW
PRESS®
A DIVISION OF THOMAS NELSON
& ZONDERVAN

WestBow Press books may be ordered through booksellers or by contacting:

WestBow Press
A Division of Thomas Nelson & Zondervan
1663 Liberty Drive
Bloomington, IN 47403
www.westbowpress.com
1 (866) 928-1240

ISBN: 978-1-5127-2018-1 (sc)
ISBN: 978-1-5127-2019-8 (hc)
ISBN: 978-1-5127-2017-4 (e)

Library of Congress Control Number: 2015919088

Print information available on the last page.

WestBow Press rev. date: 11/19/2015

Contents

Dedication

God, You are my Creator, my beginning, and my end. You are my peace, my protector, my Provider, my guide. I find my all in all in You. I thank You for Your love through Jesus Christ, my Lord. It is the greatest love I have ever known. I am in awe of You.

Steve, my husband, I am so glad that God blessed us with each other. I thank God every morning and every evening for the good man you are and for the ways in which you show your love to me. I am thankful for the way we challenge each other to do more and do better in life. You are a godsend to me. I love you, appreciate you, and respect you.

Nate (John 1:47 describes Nathanael as a man who knows no deceit), your personality has turned out to be like the description of Nathanael in Scripture. You are the reason I made up my mind never to give up in life. You have taught me so much. Through the example of your life, I have become a better person. I love you and will cherish having you for the rest of my life. I thank God for the gift of you.

Sally, my heart's princess, I pray Psalm 45:12–17. Your arrival brought healing to my heart. I found peace and fulfillment once you were born. You are strong-willed and extremely smart, yet you are also loving, caring, and full of excitement. Having you has made me stronger and more compassionate. I love you and cherish you, and I am forever thankful to God for giving you to me.

Dad, you were always my hero when I was a little girl, and you were always there in my life when I was growing up. You broke cultural barriers and raised your family in faith. You were gentle yet firm in what you believed; you did not have a need to explain yourself or to fit in. I always admired how you treated Mom, with love and respect, during a time when oppressing women was the norm. You have been such a support for me as an adult. They say that the success of a man is not measured by the money he has in the bank but by the family he has raised. In my opinion, you are an extremely successful man. I love you, Dad, and I am so glad I am your daughter.

Mama, you are my role model of what a mother and a wife should be like. You made the best of every situation, Mama. You sacrificed for your children and for many other people, and you never got tired of doing it. You treated Dad with much respect and love. You are an extremely hardworking woman, one who taught your daughters always to work hard for a better life and never to depend on anyone other than God. You raised your children in wisdom and closeness. As a result, all of your children stand together and for each other. I love you, Mama, and I am blessed to be your daughter.

My siblings, Lucy, Mary, Koome, and Isabella: each one of you has blessed my life in ways I cannot express in simple words. Growing up, we were always close, watched out for each other, and supported each other. I hold as dear many childhood memories of our times spent together: reading and trying to compose poems;

playing games like Scrabble, Monopoly, draft, and chess in the evenings; and doing a lot of talking, making jokes, and laughing. We laughed and laughed most all the time, especially because of Koome's storytelling and funny jokes. We did not have a TV until we were grown, but we were never bored for a single moment. In spite of our long distances apart as adults, we continue to be close and supportive of each other as we support our own families. I will never take any of you, or the relationship we have, for granted. I couldn't have had a better family. I love you all, and I am thankful that I am a sister to each one of you.

This book is specially dedicated to my children, Nate Munene and Sally Mwendwa, through whom God has given me the greatest responsibility I can imagine ever having. Having them has made my heart bigger, deeper, and stronger than I ever thought it would be. Because of my children, I have realized things about myself that I didn't know existed. I pray that the things Munene and Mwendwa have suffered will be a blessing and an encouragement to many. They are both awesome kids. I love them deeply, and I am blessed to be their mother.

"How do you do it!"

Forward

Nate is a very special boy whose abilities continue to exceed the expectations of everyone around him. Born with a rare brain disorder, Nate was not expected to survive and certainly not expected to learn and grow like other children. After enduring months in the hospital, numerous medications, medical nutrition therapy, and countless brain surgeries, Nate is thriving. He is learning like other kids his age, plays, does his chores at home, and is a great big brother to his little sister. Yet, Nate is still not like other children. His compassion, sensitivity and love of God are beyond his years. How did this happen? His mother, Ann Makena.

Born in Kenya, Ann Makena moved to the United States on her own as a young woman. She has endured physical, emotional and spiritual trials that most of us can't imagine. Through poetry, scripture, song and prose, Ann Makena describes how her love of the Lord and her knowledge of His plan for each of us has allowed her to be an advocate for herself and son. She knew Nate was to be her son, even when doctors told her he would not survive. She knew the Lord would provide for them, comfort them, and support them through their trials and she has been willing to follow His call. She has remained faithful. She has remained hopeful. She has remained thankful. She understands better than most of us what it truly means in the scriptures:

"I will go and do the things which the Lord commandeth, for I know that the Lord giveth no commandments unto the children of men, save he shall prepare a way for that they may accomplish the thing which He commandeth them." (Nephi 3:7)

Ann Makena and Nate are an inspiration to all of us.

By Dr. Katherine C. Nickels, M.D.
Child and Adolescent Neurology,
Mayo Clinic.

Preface

In the brokenness of my life, I have encountered God's restoring power in ways that are beyond my ability to express. This book is composed of several stories highlighting my personal testimony. The stories I share are true as I experienced them and remember them. All the names I have used of my family and friends are real. While I can't mention every person who has blessed my life, I specifically choose to mention some people, as they helped me— and I could not have made this journey on my own. The places mentioned are real. The names of some people and some places are not mentioned for privacy reasons. The stories shared in this book are only meant to encourage people who are dealing with similar situations.

All of our lives are filled with moments of joy as well as with moments of sorrow. Our experiences can be very similar and yet very different. We all can learn from one another. Since our lives can be an encouragement to one another, I am sharing my story with the hope of inspiring your life.

"How Do You Do It?"

In the last several years, the question "How do you do it and keep your sanity?" has come my way over and over. Raising my son with medical complications has been tough in the midst of my other life difficulties. My son, Nate, who is a living miracle, was not expected to survive until his birth. He was not expected to live past his first hour after being born. Nate, going on thirteen years of age today, is living an ordinary life. He overcame twenty brain surgeries, and everything that accompanied those surgeries, by age twelve. The amount of time he spent in the hospital was undeniably a lot. At age six and a half, he started a terrifying battle with seizures and had breathing emergencies, for which he had to be incubated in order to survive. His severe headaches and vomiting were among other of his life challenges.

Situations have often arisen that have caused me sorrow and shame. On the other hands, many things have happened that have caused me joy and happiness. I describe all of these things with one word: *life*.

Other than the time I've spent raising my son, which I have done with steadfastness, once my life started on a downhill path, it didn't stop going downhill for many years. Physical pain and tiredness, abuse, emotional and psychological trauma, betrayal, rejection, sleepless nights, hurts that ripped my heart, shame, and fear for my child's life, among other things, have been part of my one life. The road has been rough. It is only by God's grace that I am here today. Many people have spoken to me about life, have asked me questions, and have inspired me. The process of sharing life with others brought me to a realization that I have learned some things that might be of help to someone else along the way.

There were times when I felt very weak and did not think I had anything left in me to move my feet. Many times I felt like I would melt down in sorrow and tiredness. Some people told me how strong they thought I was. I wondered what they would think if they came close to realizing how I truly felt at such moments. I did not think of myself as strong because I knew how I had felt the many times I was called strong by others. I cried deeply when I was alone.

One day, Mac and his wife, Joan, the couple who adopted me once I moved from Kenya to the United States, visited me as I had asked them to. These two people have been one of my sets of spiritual parents for many years of my life in the United States. Having been with me through many years of suffering, they never been tired of me or were too busy for me.

During this particular evening visit, I was going through some of my most difficult moments in my life. Mac said to me, "Do you realize how strong you are?" At first, I did not want to hear that statement, especially on that day. I responded by mentioning exactly how I felt. I did not feel strong at all.

"If anything," I said, "I feel like my knees are collapsing and can't hold my weight."

Mac looked straight in my eyes and said like a dad would, in Holy Ghost anger, "Do you realize all what you have been through in the last ten years? Ann, God has given you some unique strength. I don't think you realize that! " His words came with power. I know that God spoke to me through him. At that moment, something was revealed to my heart. Mac reminded me that in spite of the things he and Joan had watched me go through, they did not see me be knocked off my feet, which Mac said was not normal. He went on to say that he believed God had given me this strength for a bigger reason than myself. I believe that God sent Mac that day to help me make sense of what never made sense to me before. That was one of the most profound evenings of my life. When Mac and Joan left that night, I was in a completely a different state than I had been in when they arrived. I began to reflect and pray in regard to the things about which Mac had spoken to me, and it became clear that the things that had gotten me through the rough waves can help get others through their struggles.

Since I have always loved writing, I found myself starting to write a book when my son was seven years old and was going through major things. This year, my son's year of restoration, has also become the year of the book completion. My suffering will not be in vain if my story is of help to someone else who is going through a tough time. I hope this book offers a voice to inspire others to fight harder for their own lives, because most good things in life don't come easy. This book gives snapshots of a continuous season of struggle in my life and shows what has been helpful to me. It is my attempt to respond to the question that has been asked to me over these years: "How do you do it?"

Acknowledgments

Were it not for God, I would not be here today. I am humbled by His goodness and mercy in my life. He has been with me through the loneliest times of my life, and He has been more faithful than I can describe. God has blessed me with the love for writing, which has always helped ease my mind. The more I know Him, the more I love Him and want to know Him more. God's grace has been with me through the writing and completing of this book.

I hold in high regard my husband Steve. He has been a support for me. Since I have met Steve, my life has been happier. We have been so good for each other and have been growing together, supporting each other, and challenging one another to become the people God has called us to be. I am thankful for Steve's understanding when I took time to complete writing this book. I am truly thankful to God for Steve in my life.

I hold in high regard my son, Nate, who has fought very hard in his young life and has kept a very positive attitude through it all. Nate has been such a source of encouragement to me. Because of him, I have started to work harder. I have learned a lot and have grown more than I had ever imagined I would. Nate's big heart of courage, resilience, thoughtfulness, and the like blow my mind daily. Nate's life is what inspired the writing of this book more than anything else. I am also very thankful for my daughter, Sally, whom God has used to bring comfort to my life. She is completely adorable and such a joy to our family. Nate and Sally are such a blessing for each other as siblings; they love each other dearly. I love my Nate and my Sally, and I am thankful for the support they have shown while I have been writing this book.

Morris, I have been blessed to have you as my own. You have been a big blessing to me, to Nate, and to Sally. I am very proud of you and of how you are handling your life at your young adult age. Thanks for cheering me on and for reading my book while I was writing it. I love you and will continue to cheer you on as you explore this big world.

I am thankful for my parents, who bore me and raised me well. I am thankful that they sacrificed two full years of their marriage for Nate's and my sake. I don't know what I would have done with them. They had faith in God and raised us, their children, in faith. They taught me from an early age that life is not easy and that it takes positive attitude and hard work to get through it. The lessons I learned by watching my mom and dad, along with the things they taught me, have contributed greatly to who I am as a person and to my ability to handle life as it comes. They made many sacrifices for their children while raising us. As adults, their love and support remains strong. It is comforting to know that they are always available for me. I am thankful for their encouragement and for believing in me as I wrote this book.

I am very thankful for my siblings Lucy, Mary, Martin, and Isabella, who have always been a source of support for me throughout my life. Sister Lucy sacrificed her family for four months when Nate was born to come to the United States and help me out—and how I needed her. Because we are close siblings, I trust Lucy, Mary, Martin, and Isabella—and I do not take them for granted. It helps to know that I have people in my life who take time to understand me and who never judge me. I am thankful that I can talk to them about anything and not fear being betrayed. Whenever I have needed anything to help me in the writing and completing of this book, they have helped me speedily. They are excited for me, which fact has been a great source of encouragement for my writing.

I am thankful for Mac and Joan, who adopted me into their family here in the United States about fourteen years ago and who have been very involved in my life. Joan has been there for me like a mom would be. She faithfully has comforted me, even at nighttime, when I have called her, and in the early morning, when I was going through several of my son's surgeries and other life situations. Mac, like a dad, has been there for me too. He challenges me to accept the gifts God has put in me. Mac and Joan are the godparents of my children, Nate and Sally. Judging by the way they support these children, I see that they take the responsibility very seriously. They have never been too busy for me. I am thankful for their support of my dreams in life and for their encouragement as I wrote this book.

I am thankful for my former employer of ten years, Hospice of the Twin Cities, as well as for my coworkers throughout my time there, for unconditional support during an extremely trying period of my life. I offer a special thanks to the people in leadership positions during my time there, especially Lisa, Becky, and Sandy. Each one of them touched my life in ways that changed me for the better—forever. My prayers remain with them. Because of their understanding, I made it through a terrible time in my life. I can't imagine how else I would have made it to this point.

I am thankful for Pastor Randy, for his many years of inspiring my life with messages of hope. His messages have been life-changing for me, especially because he teaches the Word of God very practically. I am thankful that he came to the hospital when each of my two children were born, each under difficult circumstances. He prayed for them at the beginning of their lives here on earth, and that meant a lot. I will never forget that I was a struggling student in the United States when Pastor Randy bought me a return ticket to Kenya after my nearly five years of not seeing anyone in my family. He also, along with the Speak the Word church family, financially assisted me couple times, paying half my rent when my son was hospitalized for long periods of time. I am thankful for my family of faith, i.e., the people of Speak the Word Church International, for offering many prayers for my tough life circumstances. I thank God that my pastor recognized God's calling on my life when I had nothing to show for it and also that he has supported me in it. I am thankful that Pastor Randy did not forsake me when I fell and, according to the world, was supposed to be forsaken. I am thankful for the many times he encouraged me to pursue my dreams of writing, of composing, and of helping orphans in Kenya, among other things. Thank you, Pastor Randy, for making such a difference in my life and in the life of my family.

I am thankful to all the hospitals where Nate has received medical care. A special thanks to Children's Hospital Minneapolis for providing great care and safety during my son's early years. Thanks to all staff members there who touched my child's life and made it better. Thanks for the support I received during the tough times.

I hold as very special in my heart the doctors who have played a very big role in saving and caring for Nate's life, from the doctors who delivered him very safely to those in whose care he remains. A special thanks goes to Dr. Susan Maleh of Partners in Pediatrics, who was Nate's primary doctor until she retired, in Nate's eleventh year. Dr. Maleh was an amazing doctor for both Nate and Sally at delicate times of each of their lives. Nate has been blessed with some of the most amazing doctors, surgeons, neurologists, and nurses. Although I do not mention every name here, I am very thankful for each one of them. Thank you for being a support to us as a family in times of need. Thank you for the education you gave us when we were under your care. I consider that each of you plays a part in this story.

I am very thankful to the staff at Neurosurgical Associates, Minneapolis, for the support given to my son during his early years of life. A very special thanks goes to the surgeon Dr. Nagib for operating on my son at very delicate times and for keeping him safe each and every time he underwent an operation. Nate was only five days old when Dr. Nagib first operated on his brain, which fact never ceases to amaze me. Dr. Nagib's compassion and dedication is amazing. My family all hold him very dear to our hearts for helping save Nate's life. Today, I have a story to inspire others because of his great contribution.

I am thankful to Gillette Children's Specialty Healthcare in St. Paul for excellent neurology care and therapy sessions whenever Nate needed it, and also for doing Nate's neuropsychological evaluation. Thanks to all the staff members who have been involved in Nate's care. I am thankful especially to the neurologist Dr. Brenningstell Gillen for his great care and support of Nate, for believing in me as a mother, and for referring Nate to the Mayo Clinic, where he felt Nate could get the best help. Thank you for continuing to call on a regular basis to check on Nate. He feels really special and happy whenever you call. I will always esteem you for being supportive of me at very difficult times with Nate, for getting to the bottom of what needed to be done for him, and for following through.

I am specially thankful to the Mayo Clinic in Rochester for believing in miracles. I have been amazed by the culture of faith at the Mayo Clinic and by the fact that the staff there put out their best effort for Nate. The Mayo Clinic, in my opinion, is a place where God is given a stage to work in His people's lives. The staff there are full of grace. I am thankful to the Mayo Clinic for the excellent care and the medical success story of my son, Nate. Thank you for believing in me as a mother and for listening to me with respect and understanding as I described my son's experience of life. Thank you for helping Nate from his points of strength, not from his points of weakness. Thank you for the surgeries and the medical therapy that you considered for Nate and subsequently controlled until he thrived. Thank you for the great compassion shown to Nate and to us as a family throughout this journey. For the first time in Nate's entire life, we have had at least a year and half of zero ER visits and zero hospitalizations, which is a miracle. Nate's struggle with seizures, which started before he turned seven years old and got worse over time, has been resolved since he started going to the Mayo Clinic in the fall of 2011. Since before mid-2014 to date, which is more than a year and half, Nate has not had seizures in spite of his medications being reduced to minimal. A very special thanks goes to the neurologist Dr. Katherine C. Nickels, the neurosurgeon Dr. Nicholas Wetjen, and the dietitian Susan Eckert, among others, for their dedication to Nate's life and for their support of my family.

I am thankful for my sister-in-law Linda, who read this book when I started putting pieces of it together and who gave me insights that helped shape it.

I am thankful to Reggie Cammon, who helped me with my internship process many years ago under my pastor, Randy. Reggie also helped me greatly by making corrections to this book. Reggie has a degree in journalism; as such, his advice has been very valuable, as has his time spent on correcting parts of this book. Reggie's encouragement and guidance also helped ease my mind and let me enjoy my summer with my children, which meant the world to my children and to me at the end of summer.

A very special thanks goes to Dr. Katherine Nickels, Pediatric and Adolescent Medicine, Mayo Clinic. I loved her from the day I went to the Mayo Clinic for Nate's first appointment. She listens with her heart, which is a most valuable trait. I went home on day one with a knowing that all was going to be okay with my son. That's how she made me feel. She then left no stone unturned in helping my child, for which I cannot thank her enough. My heart and my family hold a very special place in our hearts for her because of the person she is—other than being an excellent neurologist. Dr. Katherine C. Nickels has also supported and contributed greatly to my work of writing. I am thankful to her for reading through this book, and for writing a foreword consisting of a medical summary of Nate's treatment at the Mayo Clinic. Dr. Nickels' foreword is very touching and humbling to my heart. I am so very thankful to her for believing in me and for supporting me in the ways that have changed my child's life and my own life forever.

Special thanks go to my friend Agnes, who is like a sister, for the many times she kept my child (or both of my children) for several days at a time or for a week while I was tending to another child. Agnes, you kept them all when Steve and I went for honey. You have never been afraid of dealing with any medical complications. Each and every time, you handled the situation with grace. Sometimes, in spite of your own struggles, you took time off work to help me out, because you took Nate seriously. For this, I will forever be thankful for you. I have been blessed by the relationship your sons, Matthew and Osteen, have maintained with Nate all their lives. Matthew and Osteen have always been very kind to and patient with Nate when he has had struggles. The three together have always been like brothers. When I ended up having an emergency C-section at Sally's birth and was fighting for my life in the hospital, you dropped everything to care for Nate. You are one of the most blessed women I know. I love you deeply. I thank God for bringing you into my life.

Special thanks go to Jennifer and John for keeping my daughter three full weeks while I was going through an intense time with Nate's treatment. Sally was not yet two years old when you opened your home to her (and Morris). You sacrificed plenty of your work time to help me out. You drove many miles several times within those three weeks to bring Sally to the Mayo Clinic so that she could see her brother and me. You loved Sally like your own. She had such a great time with your children Shiru, Colleen, and Silas. I will never forget the fact that she was calling you Mom and Dad by the end of the three weeks. You also sacrificed so much for my family many other times. I remember when Nate was little and you carried your three little children to the hospital—even when I told you not to come. You have such a big heart and are a blessed family. We love you and thank God for you.

Special thanks go to Alice for the many days Nate spent in her house while I worked. Thanks to Sam, Alice's son, for his friendship to Nate. Sam has been friends with Nate since they both were about a year old. Thanks to Alice's mom for watching Nate and for seeing the gift he is. After my mom went back to Kenya, when Nate was four and half, Alice's mother watched Nate when he was not at school so that I could go to work. She pointed out things about Nate that I had always taken for granted. She let me know how generous and kind Nate is. She watched other children, and she let me that Nate was the child who watched to ensure that the other children were being fair. She said Nate would not eat anything if the other children were not eating. She said Nate had to share what he had no matter how little it was. That meant a lot to me, because it describes Nate's personality, confirming that which God had laid in my heart about him before he was born.

A special thanks to my cousins Eric and Duncan, who happened to be single. Especially during my life as a single mother, they stepped up to the plate and provided the male support for Nate that he really needed. My mind holds images of Nate as a little boy climbing all over Uncle Duncan and wrestling with him almost on a daily basis. Duncan, who was my childhood neighbor, became like a real brother during the time of my and Nate's life when we needed him the most. That will never be forgotten. My cousin Eric, although he had a drive, took time often to come and spend time with us. I have images of Nate and Uncle Eric in the swimming pool as well as of Nate tucked in very close, almost under Uncle Eric's armpit. Eric and Duncan both made such a difference in Nate's life during the time of his greatest struggles. They continue to be a blessing whenever they can. God bless them and their families.

I am thankful for many other family members and friends, and for the people who have touched my children's lives as well as my life deeply during these several years of struggle. Some visited us in the hospital each and every time without fail and brought us food. Some visited us at home, and others helped watch my kids so I could go to work. Some came together and raised money to support us when my hospital stays with my son were long. Some came to sit with me and my children during the tough times and helped me around my home while I was sick. Some prayed with us regularly and made phone calls to check on us. Although I was not able to send a thank-you card to every person, my heart holds more gratitude than words can express. More than ten years of my life have been extremely difficult. My life would not have been the same without each of these people in my life.

A special thanks to LoveWorks Academy in Minneapolis, which was Nate's school from kindergarten to third grade. Nate was young and delicate when he started school, but the staff there made me feel comfortable enough to leave him with them. I felt they all cared greatly for Nate and watched out for him like their own. Nate started having seizures the summer before he started second grade, which really complicated his life. He was started on ant seizure medications that totally changed how he functioned at that time. The principal of LoveWorks Academy, Mrs. Harrison, and the teachers took the change extremely well and continued to watch out for Nate. He had big seizures while at school, and he underwent multiple hospitalizations with multiple brain surgeries. The people at LoveWorks never gave up on him or treated him differently. They provided accommodations for him as the school was able—and with a lot of grace. Nate felt very loved the entire time he was at LoveWorks Academy. I was a single mother at the time, and I felt very supported and was treated with respect the entire time Nate attended classes there. A special thanks to Mrs. Harrison, Mrs. Guzman, Mrs. Monsaas, and Mrs. Alberts, all who worked with Nate very directly most of the time. A special thanks also goes to the nurse Jenifer of Minnesota Visiting Nurse Agency (MVNA), who provided support for Nate as well as for me. A special thanks to Ms. Cade kenatia, who placed calls to me and received calls from me—and was always supportive and very pleasant. A special thanks to Mrs. Stewart, who kept Nate in her class for two years. She showed great compassion and talent in the way she worked with him during a very complicated time of his life. A special thanks to Mr. Jeff DeWitt, who also taught Nate during a complicated time of his life and who did very great with him. Mr. DeWitt also sacrificed a lot of his time, mileage, and gas during the summer of 2012, as he came to our home regularly, at least twice a week, to coach Nate. Nate had gone through the biggest brain surgery he had ever had, in April 2012, and was taking time to recover, which left him behind at school. Mr. DeWitt and his wife, Kelly, also took some trips to the Mayo Clinic while Nate was hospitalized. This meant the world to Nate and to our family. After Mr. DeWitt and his family moved out of state, he continued to be a hero for Nate, checking on him regularly. We love Mr. DeWitt. We will always cherish the five years that Nate spent at LoveWorks Academy. As time has gone by, we realize more what a special place it was for Nate and stress free for mom.

A thank you from the bottom of my heart goes to West Bow Press for their guidance throughout my process of completing this book and for publishing it.

Introduction

Makena is my given name. This name was given to me by my loving parents at my birth. Their prayer for my life was that I would be a bringer of joy.

From a Safe Nest to Tumbling Waves

The village is a wonderful place to raise children. I come from Meru, Kenya. My parents are called Joseph and Dorothy. I am remarried to Steve. I am the mother of Nate and Sally, whose names will be mentioned throughout this book. When Steve and I got married, Nate was 8years old and Sally was less than a year old. I also raised my nephew Morris a great deal as my own son. He is in college. My first marriage separated when Nate was two years old and ended in divorce. I have two brothers and two sisters. Koome, my younger brother, has his own family. My sisters, Lucy and Mary, are twins; they have their own families as well. Morris, who was our firstborn brother, died suddenly when he was twenty-five years old. I have a cousin named Isabella, to whom my siblings and I refer to as our sister because she was mostly raised with us. I was raised in a stable home. Although my mother and father were married at the young ages of sixteen and twenty-two, respectively, they always loved each other dearly and supported each other when they were raising us. They are still married and are happy together, fifty-three years later.

I went to boarding school when I was eleven years old, which was normal for many Kenyans at the time. That meant I was at school for about three months at a time. I took a one-month break from school each year to be home with my family. While my older siblings academically topped their respective classes, I did not get good grades, which was hard for my family. I was very involved in drama, creative writing, choir, drama, poetry, and leadership. I knew from an early age that God's call on my life was to minister to His people. Although I went to Kenya's national level with some of these activities, I was not celebrated by my family, because what mattered was high academic performance. I carried sadness for having been in boarding school against my wishes and for being compared to my sisters regularly, which I believe affected my academic performance to some degree. I did not talk much about my feelings growing up because I knew without a doubt that my parents and my family loved me and wanted what they believed was best for me. I often felt frustrated, because the things that mattered to me did not matter to anyone else—yet I could not shake these things off to please my family, no matter how hard I tried. I could not understand why I was forced to study geography, chemistry, and physics in class when no one cared about my love for poetry, speaking, drama, writing, and composition. Not many people made it with these kind of talents in Kenya, but something kept pressing in my spirit. What was expected was getting an education and then getting a job after school or college, and that is what parents generally pushed for. Although I did not like being in boarding school, it gave me the opportunity to get involved in what I liked best without always having to talk about it with my parents, and it also made me stronger at a young age.

Apart from my family's lack of support for my interests, my family relationships were close and strong while I was growing up.

They remain strong now that I am an adult, in spite of the physical distances between me and my family members. As I got older, my desires for my future became stronger, although some of what I wanted was unattainable because of the reality of my natural life at the time. One of the wildest dreams I had was one of going to the United States, where people are able to develop their talents. To my family and other people I knew, this was the craziest dream they had ever heard me mention. They wondered what I was thinking and how I was thinking I could get to the United States.

The day came when I finally found myself at Chicago O'Hare International Airport (USA), which was my dream of many years come true. Little did I know that my life was going to be changed in ways that were never expected.

While at O'Hare, I all of a sudden realized I was alone, completely alone! Traveling from Kenya through Germany, changing planes, and having to take shuttles in Germany was all scary, but it was quick and people helped me. It was interesting being around so many people who spoke in English like I did, but it took forever for us to understand each other. So I didn't speak much to people in the planes or during the layovers. It didn't bother me that I had no one to talk to, because I had too much to absorb. Besides, I had a destination that I could not wait to get to: the United States of America! Finally, there I was standing in that huge airport with no one to turn to. My having come from the village lifestyle of Kenya did not help. I was filled with emotions: excitement, amazement, happiness, shock, fear—you name it. I did not know what to think. At first I just stopped and watched. Everyone was moving so fast, with their heads high and looking straight ahead, and no one seemed to stop or look sideways. Most people just walked until they disappeared out of my sight. No one seemed to speak to anyone else. The more I watched, the more my excitement was replaced by panic. I had no dad, no mom, no sisters, and no brother to call! I was on my own for the first time in my entire life—and in a huge foreign country.

What next? I thought. I looked around for uniformed people, found some, and approached one. I tried to explain to him where I was coming from and where I was going. At that time, there were no cell phones, so he directed me to a pay phone and gave me directions for how to place a call to the school to which I was going. I had exchanged my money from Kenya shillings to US dollars, but I had no idea what the dollars meant in terms of how to spend the money. When I got to the pay phone, I found myself totally confused. I was already frustrated with trying to explain myself, so I stood there and waited. Eventually, one woman who was coming to make a call noticed me. I am sure I looked puzzled and lost. She asked me if I needed help. I said yes, explaining to her where I had come from and stretching out my hand with money so that she could take what she needed to help me place the call. Asking me to put my money in my pocket, she used her money to make my call. No one picked up the phone, so she handed me the receiver to leave a voice mail message. I had no idea what that meant. She was a wonderful person. In spite of the dynamics between us, she was patient and gave me guidance. She was one of those angels God sends along the way. I experienced her for a short time, but I still hold her dear to my heart. I got to school safely; however, by the time I arrived, nothing seemed fun. I was super exhausted, feeling sad and confused, and all I wanted to do was cry. So I did cry.

For me, coming to the United States was a faith-based deal, but I found out fairly quickly that living by faith is not as easy as I had thought it would be. Life can be wonderful, but before you know it, it's going downhill very fast and very out of control. Having come from a stable family, and with no experience of being on my own, I wasn't prepared for figuring out for myself what life had to offer. Because I had never had to work much for anything, I had the assumption that life always worked out easily. In a rude awakening, I found out how erroneous my thinking was.

I was in my early twenties when I left my parents' home with their blessing—and with their help to pursue my life's dreams in the United States. I did not know anyone closely. I was faced with figuring out everything about my new life in a foreign country all by myself. It was much harder than I had imagined. But this was now my life, and I had to do it.

I remember the below-freezing days of my first winter as I waited for the buses to take me, with no winter clothes, to school. I remember walking to work for my night shifts, which began at 11:00 p.m. I remember the chill in my heart upon hearing the gunshots go off in downtown Minneapolis as I waited for the buses. All I could do was pray, trust God, and keep moving, because I did not want to quit. I went through some major brokenness during that season of my life. Everything seemed very tough to me, but God's grace got me through it. I also remember funny experiences like asking an American for directions to downtown Minneapolis. It went like this: "Take a left and then the first right. Walk two blocks, and then take another left. Take another right. You will see your bus stop on the left." By the time the person was done, I had forgotten what he had first said. So I asked him to repeat the directions. While he did so, I committed only the first turn to memory and blocked out everything else after that. Every turn I made, I stopped to ask someone else for directions, until I reached my bus stop.

In my adult life, I have had many reasons to give up. In addition to the struggle I experienced in relocating to the United

States, I have suffered abuse, rejection, shame, betrayal—you name it. I have been divorced, been a single mother, had a near death experience, and raised my child whose medical conditions were so grave that hospitals were like home to us. I have been in wrong relationships, which left me more heartbroken than I had been before entering them. I have been judged, misrepresented, slandered, and looked down on. But among the hardness of life, God sent people to support me and to encourage me through thick and thin. Although there have been many times when I felt like life was never going to get better, I chose to pay attention to the glimpses of hope that came into my life. Learning to listen to the voice of God, and to those He sent to encourage me, is what has gotten me this far through my life circumstances.

As a woman and mother, I have gone through a process that has led me to take my role seriously. Growing up, I had many culturally specific experiences that made me believe I was not a woman until I was married and had children. I also believed that I would not be a good woman if I were ever divorced or abandoned by a man. It was not easy to erase those messages. I have made wrong choices and have put myself in worse situations than God intended for me because of these beliefs. When I was growing up, women who were not married at a certain age were ridiculed. People talked ill of them, even stating that something must be wrong with them. Many other women lived with abuse and oppression and would never leave their husband for their children's sake—but also for fear of losing the status of being a good woman. These and many other beliefs were ingrained in my mind very strongly. When I grew up, I could not get myself to step into my calling because my mind told me I had to get married first to be complete. The struggles I have endured on account of my wrong beliefs left me heartbroken and fragmented. I thank

God that, because of His love, He picked up my broken pieces and put them back together. He has over time revealed to me many truths about who He made me to be through His Word. He also made my heart whole again. He helped me understand that I am a complete woman because He made me complete, and that I need nothing outside of me to complete me. I have seen the Lord bless my life since I became satisfied with who I am in Him. As a mother, I receive my children from God, realizing that parenting is the toughest job. My goal is to raise them in the light of God. Of any ministry work to which God has called me, my children are the first responsibility on the list. God made my heart secure in being a woman and a mother. Those are the two most important responsibilities in my life.

In my ministry work, I have a heart for people, especially in their times of pain and suffering. My mother was a social worker and is very kind at heart. I watched her tirelessly help the people in a community who were less privileged than she. She made sacrifices for others without looking down on anyone because of their problem, whatever it may have been. Many times after she came home from work, she would go to look after elderly neighbors who were neglected. She gave them the care they needed, including washing their bodies and washing their clothes by hand. Starting when I was young, she took me with her during my school holidays. I believe in the process: her heart for helping others inspired my calling. From an early age, I was usually in tune with the suffering of others, even when I could not relate to their circumstances. The suffering I have endured has helped me relate to people more and has refined my desire to help others. Today I can look back and truly say that everything I have been through has made me a better person. I have become more accepting of other people's journeys. I have stopped judging other people's situations. I've learned to accept God's grace and mercy when I am wrong, which is very humbling, because there is nothing I can do to pay back His love through Jesus Christ. Forgiving myself and accepting myself as God forgave me and accepted me has helped me in forgiving others and accepting others. I have come to conclude that no matter what happens, life isn't hopeless until we give up on ourselves!

Introducing Nate and Sally

My Inspiration

Nathanael and Munene are his given names. "Nathanael" in Hebrew means, "God has given" or "gift of God." "Munene" is a Meru name meaning "a leader." These names are a confession of my prayers and blessings for my son's life. In my family, we refer to Nathanael as Nate, which is the name used for him in this book. His name was placed in my heart while I was reading John 1:43–51. When I found out I was pregnant, the impression came to my heart again: "Nathanael." It was so clear that I started calling the child by his name before the ultrasound confirmed I had a boy in my womb. However, there was an attack on his life, so with the ultrasound came a bad report. Nathanael was found to have brain complications and was not expected to survive to term. If by any chance he did, he was not expected to live for even an hour after his birth. As the doctors spoke to me about their expectations based on the brain images, I saw Nathaniel, in my spirit, crying, walking, talking, playing, and growing. I decided to follow my heart and to leave Nate's fate to God. By God's grace, Nate had his own mind—and he decided to live and thrive. Although my son's young life has not been easy, God has been faithful and has never forsaken us. Nate's development as a baby was miraculous, as he was not expected to function like other children, yet he was not late for any milestone. In spite of his multiple brain surgeries, which had reached a total of at least seven by the time he was three years old, he did everything a child his age should do. He ate, crawled, stood, walked, talked, and was potty-trained at an age-appropriate time, which compelled me to fight for his life even more. I remember when he turned two years old. His pediatrician, Susan, said to me, "Nate is a normal child and should be treated as normal." Even though I knew Nate to be a child who was unlike other children, given his level of functioning, it was nice to hear those words from his doctor, because that prognosis was not medically expected.

Nate spent a lot of time in hospitals because of the complications with his brain. No one seemed to know what caused what. Anytime he had any symptoms, he was hospitalized in order to be monitored and checked.

Nate attended LoveWorks Academy, a charter school, at the appropriate age. He learned like other children. In fact, he was very smart. He learned in a regular classroom setting and brought home A's until he developed seizures, just as he was starting second grade at seven years old. For the first time in his life, he was put on medications, which disoriented him greatly and which led to allergic reactions, numerous hospitalizations, and additional brain surgeries. It was at that time that I noticed some decline in his function, although it did not last long. He did bounce back. Academically, he was affected and needed more help, although he continued to learn and show progress. The struggle with seizures became worse, even life-threatening, with a lot of allergies from medications leading to struggles with breathing or not breathing altogether. It was also during this most stressful time of my life that I got pregnant with Nate's sister, Sally. By the time Nate turned eight years old and was struggling immensely, Sally, having just recently been born, was only three months old.

After I endured a lot of struggle and a search for answers, the Lord lead me online to discover more treatments for seizures, ones that Nate had not received. I discussed these with his neurologist at the time, Dr. Brenningstell, who decided the best thing to do was to refer Nate to the Mayo Clinic. Nate was nine years old, struggling with bad seizures, medications, and allergies. By the time he went to the Mayo Clinic, there was nothing more left to do for him other than to feed him medications and let things take their course. Once he was a patient at the Mayo Clinic, many tests were run and a decision was made to do a major brain surgery to extract the part of his brain causing the bad seizures. After that surgery was performed, Nate had another surgery, to revise the shunt. He was put on Ketogenic diet for about two and half years.

I thank God for confirming the word of His that He put in my heart concerning Nate before he was born. I don't know what is in Nate's future, just like I don't know what is in my future. But there is one thing I know for sure, and that is that Nate's life is in God's hands. Many people raise children with not a single struggle and then something happens all of a sudden that changes everything. This tells me that no one really knows what to expect of any child. Many of us live in hope and prayer for our children. I have raised my son daily by faith, not knowing what to expect and fully trusting God for him. God has given me the peace that passes understanding. Nate's personality is that of the man who knows no deceit, who fully trusts God. Our God has made ways in the wilderness and rivers in the desert places for this journey. He has made me into a much better person. Some people along the way have asked me why Nate endured so much suffering when

God had spoken concerning Nate. God did not promise me that having Nate was going to be easy. What He promised was to be with me—and that He has been.

> But now, thus says the Lord, who created you, O Jacob, And He who formed you, O Israel: "Fear not, for I have redeemed you; I have called *you* by your name; You *are* Mine. When you pass through the waters, I *will be* with you; And through the rivers, they shall not overflow you. When you walk through the fire, you shall not be burned, Nor shall the flame scorch you. For I *am* the Lord your God, The Holy One of Israel, your Savior." (Isaiah 43:1–3 ESV)

In the midst of the suffering, I saw God at work in our lives day by day. I did what I had to do and held my peace about it only because I had learned to depend on God every step of the way. God put me in places no one else could have put me in. He sustained me even when I was unsustainable. I believe that God spoke to the people to whom He needed to speak on my behalf, because He knew my circumstances. How many mornings I had to clean up vomit and change clothing right as we were getting ready to leave the house to go to school and work. How many times I started the journey to school and ended up in the ER. How many times I was at work and was called to go pick up my child from school. How many times my son was hospitalized, some of those hospitalizations lasting up to a month at a time. I was late for work almost regularly for the period of time when my son was on a Ketogenic diet. Although my company supported me, I was very aware that not everyone wanted me there. Yet I never worried, not for one single day, that I was going to lose my job, because deep in my heart God put such reassurance. He knew the details of my life and told me that my children and I were going to be okay. What kind of company keeps a person like me for ten years unless God is involved? That is one example, among the many other things I saw God do, of something that humbled my heart and taught me never to be afraid of His call, no matter how difficult things seem. I have seen God work in mysterious ways like He did in His Word. The way in which He works cannot make sense to our minds. I have learned that trying to understand how God will work things out makes me miss out on Him. When God gave His children Jericho, He instructed them to lift up a shout so that the walls around the city would fall flat on the ground to let them into the land (Joshua 6). What sense did that make in that situation? When the enemies came against the Israelites one way, God dispersed them seven ways. He provided His children with manna in the wilderness. All that Moses had to do was to touch the sea with his walking stick so that it would part and let the Israelites through. These works exemplify the God I have come to trust, because He is the same God today.

When I read the Bible, I also see many people who suffered greatly even though God had called them or spoken to them concerning their lives, including Jesus, my Lord. Moses was called to deliver the children of Israel, but it did not happen without pain. We live in a fallen world, and as long as we live we will have trials, because the Enemy is always at war with the human race. What really matters to me is to know I am here for God's purpose—and only God knows when a person has fulfilled his or her purpose. Reading the Word of God and praying, as well as having the support of many people, has kept me going thus far. Even though it has not been easy for me and my family, it has been amazing to watch God work out the details for Nate's sake.

Nate is twelve years old and has not had a seizure in at least year and half. He successfully recovered from about twenty brain surgeries and is now starting seventh grade. His life has been more stable in the last year than I had ever imagined it would be. For this I praise God. We have had no ER visits, no hospitalizations, and no doctor's constant calls about one thing or another; instead, we have had a quiet, peaceful life for more than a year now. Nate has a deep, strong faith, and he loves to memorize and recite Scriptures. Even during the most stressful times of his life, he always remembers to pray and to ask for prayers. Nate's personality is gentle, loving, attentive, and very caring. He watches out for others and protects those who need help. He is a gift to all those who get to know him. He is eager to learn life skills. Even at his age, he does the dishes and his laundry as well as some cooking and cleaning. Nate is a junior board member for an organization that is raising money to build homes for orphans in Kenya. He does chores in order to give a portion of all the money he gets, including gifts, to this organization. He also loves art and draws copies of pictures that look like the original. He hopes to make art a career, but he is also open to God's leading. Other than being an amazing son, Nate is a wonderful older brother to Sally. The two get along very well. They love each other, read together, play together, and watch out for each other. It is such a blessing that they have each other.

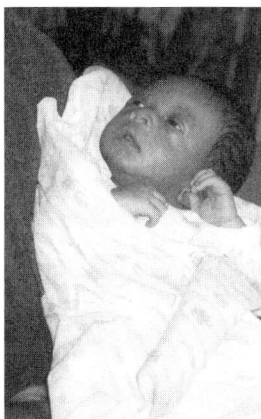

Baby Nate

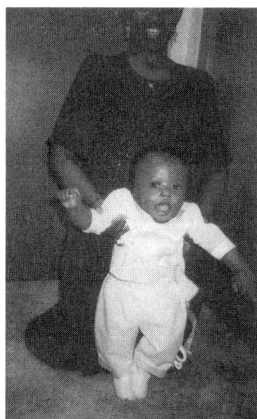

Day of dedication

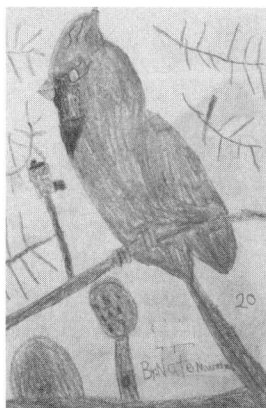

Drawn by Nate
without tracing

Nate as a student at
LoveWorks Academy

Thank God for
the Mayo Clinic

Jehovah is El-Shaddai, and
He still works miracles.

My Blessing

Sally and Mwendwa are her given names.

Since naming a child is one of the most important things to me, I chose my daughter's names as my prayers of blessings for her life. "Sally" in Hebrew means "princess," and "Mwendwa" is a Meru name for girls meaning "loved one." In one sentence, Sally is "Princess, loved one" or "loved princess." My belief is that this confession over my daughter overcomes every attack sent against her life by anyone throughout her entire life. She is completely special, loved, and blessed. God has her here for His purpose. Sally and Nate are a great support for each other. I am so glad they have each other as siblings.

Sally weighed about two pounds at birth. She was very tiny, yet she was also beautiful and perfect. Although her heart rate was dropping fast right before she was born, she did very well once she was delivered. She was able to eat right away. She breathed without any intervention and did not have any complications at all. I believe that God had mercy on my situation, because Sally was born during a time when I was going through tough situations with Nate. Two weeks before Sally was born, Nate had a medical emergency where he had a prolonged seizure and, with treatment, quit breathing. Sally was born during an extremely chaotic period of my life. She was ready to be discharged one week after she was born, as she had no medical condition that would keep her in the hospital. The doctor said that her being tiny was not a reason to keep her, but they were gracious to keep her for one more week, giving me time to adjust for her care at home. This was another instance of God's grace, because I was sick from preeclampsia and was taking care of myself and of my son, Nate.

I'll never forget the first time I saw Sally. Even though I was heavily medicated after the C-section, I clearly remember her wide-open eyes that stared into my eyes like she knew everything and was full of wisdom. I remember wishing I could have a conversation with her. I wondered what she was thinking. I couldn't wait to hold her in my arms, but I wasn't able to do so until the following day. I am very thankful for my pastor, who went to pray for Sally while she was still in the hospital. God's Word tells us to call the elders of the church for prayer. I believe there was power released upon Sally's life when Pastor Randy prayed over her. Two weeks after she was born, Sally was discharged to me. She weighed about three pounds. She was so tiny that she wore a doll dress home, one that was brought to her by my friend Jennifer. I was blessed to have caring people in my life, like my cousin Eric and my friend Ann, who came to the hospital with me to help bring Sally home and get things settled at home. Other friends came to check on us at home regularly, which I will forever be thankful for.

Although I was still recovering, I had my two children looking up to me. I had to pick myself up. Although it was not easy, I did just fine. God was so gracious that the first two months after Sally was born, Nate somehow did not have any seizures. Those were two months when I needed him to hold together most, because I was still recovering from high blood pressure and a C-section. On top of that, Sally was too delicate to ride in a vehicle. During those two months of recovery, I also saw God intervene with my coworkers. For almost the entire two months that I was sick, someone from work brought me food. This happened every day. I did not cook for the entire time I was sick. Some of my coworkers also came to spend time with me and my children. Some brought many gifts for my children. How do you describe this kind of goodness?! Hospice of the Twin Cities, my workplace, was an expression of God's unconditional love for me at a time I needed it the most. For this I hold a lot of gratitude in my heart.

God had mercy and blessed Sally and Nate with Steve for a dad when Sally was less than a year old. Sally continued to grow very well. She only went to the doctor for her scheduled appointments. She has, however, spent a lot of time in the hospitals beside her brother, Nate. Also, she has experienced some trauma resulting from her brother's medical condition. What is it like for a baby, or a two-year-old, to watch her brother have seizures over and over, to see him have Band-Aids on his head after surgeries, to watch him lying down and groaning in pain! That was the environment in which Sally grew for the first few years of her life, before Nate's condition stabilized. She happens to be extremely smart and talented, but she was also exposed to an environment that most children aren't exposed to, which, I think, caused her to grow up fast.

In raising Sally, I kept my mind aware of her even when I was preoccupied with tough situations with Nate. I intentionally gave her attention, knowing that it was easy for me to be very caught up in her brother's care. Keeping in mind that she was the baby, I communicated that fact to her. Her lovable nature is a blessing. I have raised Sally in faith. She learned to pray and talk simultaneously. I started reading to her God's Word and kids' stories from day one. God had blessed Sally in unique ways. When she was three years old, she memorized each of her storybooks after hearing them read about three times. She would open the book and recite the whole story page by page, without missing a single word. She was four years old when we (as a family) realized she was actually reading books and asking for help with some big words. By the time Sally turned five years old, she could pick up any book, including the Bible, and read even big words, needing (very little) help with complex words only. We had to test her by giving her different books to read, including schoolbooks, to ascertain the fact that she was indeed reading by five years of age. She loves reading and never needs to be reminded to read. The one time I put Sally in time-out, I found her happily reading her books in her bedroom instead of thinking about why she was there.

Sally plays a lot, is full of imagination, and likes to investigate many things she comes across. Very caring and gentle-spirited, she likes to take care of others. She learns very fast and it is a challenge to keep her occupied enough. She knows what she wants and can push boundaries sometimes. For example, I went through a season of bedtime struggle right around the time when she turned five. She did not want to sleep when it was bedtime. Every night after I read with her and tucked her in, she would find a reason to come back downstairs five minutes after I left her room. It was a different reason each day, and she often gave a reason that was difficult to challenge. The moment I started walking back toward her bedroom with her, she would get excited and start telling me stories. I realized that her need was to talk, not the cold, the hurt, or the hunger of which she had originally complained.

At the time of this writing, Sally is five years old, ready for kindergarten. At home, Sally and Nate play together, read together, and do chores together. They are great advocates for each other, and they love each other dearly. My prayer is that they will always be close while they are growing up and that they will continue to support each other in their adult lives. I am thankful that Sally and Nate have each other. I thank God every day for bringing Sally into my life and for the joy she brings to me. She is amazing to be around. I am so happy to be her mother.

With my daughter, Sally

Baby Sally, at about three pounds, going home

Day of dedication

Sally with her big brother

Reading together

Sally at four years old

Off to kindergarten

What Inspired Me to Write This Book

In my mind, I still hear the loud cries of my child in the midst of having auras (colorful images in his brain resulting from the electrical charges that cause his seizures) before the attacking seizures manifested. I still hear him calling softly, "Help, Mom," as he ran fast in confusion, trying to locate me. I still feel my heart beating with terror, fearing what could happen if he fell and hit his head. I remember times when I flew up the stairs to hold him so that he didn't reach the end of the staircase and roll down it. Life was almost a constant run whenever he was not sitting right next to me. I remember fighting thoughts and fear as I handed him over to the surgeons for each of his twenty brain surgeries. I wondered, each time, if that was the last time I'd see my son breathe. Each time, I waited in a paralyzed state, not wanting to think of what to expect when the surgeons came to talk to me after each of the surgeries.

Life generally comes with many challenges. There is not a single person on earth who has never faced a challenge of some sort. Some people have more struggles than others. Some people have had to deal with major life circumstances. I don't know where I rank, but I have been in situations that have made me feel like my knees were turning into jelly and would not hold my weight. I have had moments when I felt very alone and lost. I have made both good and bad choices. Many times, I have been asked a question by those who have known some of what my life has been like: "How do you do it?" It is this question that has caused me to reflect on my life's journey.

My greatest reason for writing this book is to give glory and honor to God for what He has done in my family's life. There is no way my son would be alive—and not only alive but also living like other children his age—had it not been for God's hand on his life. There is no way I would have made it this far and remained sane were it not for the grace of God. My hope is that those who read this book will be inspired to face life with faith and courage in spite of negative past and present circumstances. I hope that this testimony will help you to cast off the limits you have set for yourself and the limit of what God can do for you. God wants to bless your life. Are you willing and ready to receive all He has in store for you?

Another thing that inspired me to write this book was my realization that many things are left undone because of the assumption that someone else has done it or will do it. I made a decision to live up to my calling and to encourage others to live up to their calling. We all have room to inspire one another with stories of what God has done in our lives or to bless one another in many other ways if we put fear aside.

Part One

I Dare to Dream

Dreams do come true

Wherever you can see yourself in the Spirit, you can be in the natural.

Born and raised in the small village of Meru, Kenya, I believed that my coming to America was an unattainable dream in the natural. America was for the very rich people of Kenya and the rest of the world, not for rural people like me. During my years of middle school, I was in a boarding school called St. Peter's Ishiara in the Embu district of Kenya. I had friends who came from Nairobi, the capital of Kenya, and some of those friends were from rich families. When I first met many of these people, I discovered that they had had a lot more exposure to the world than I had. As they talked about their expectations of life after school, my way of thinking started to resemble their way of thinking. I started to think big.

When I went home for holidays after every three months at school, I started talking to my parents and siblings about my new dreams. I remember my dad laughing his heart out and calling me a dreamer, like he always did. My family had fun listening to me talk as well as evaluating the rich people we knew who lived in America. We laughed about my ideas. As far as our family was concerned, I did not compare to any of those who had made it. But while we talked and laughed about my dream to move to America, my dream was becoming more and more real to my spirit. I started wondering, *Why not? My rich friends and I all have the same God.* I went to Nguviu Girls' High School in Embu, Kenya, and continued to believe that I was meant to live in America. My parents changed from laughing at me to being afraid for me.

My parents are strong believers in education. After I finished high school, they placed me in Meru Technical Institute, where

I pursued a two-year education in basic accounting. This was against my will, but I did it in obedience to my parents. While I went to college, I struggled with my parents, asking them to help me go to America. They did not know how; it was beyond their ability. Daddy said I could enroll in any college in Kenya that I wanted to attend, because I did not want to be an accountant. From an early age, I knew deeply in my heart that I had a calling to be in ministry and to engage in people's related affairs, although I didn't know exactly how I would do these things. So I set out to search for a college that would prepare me for ministry.

Although I was supposed to find a college in Nairobi, my statement changed from "I dream of America" to "I am going to America." By this time, I had a knowing in my heart, one that I could not turn off. I was excited, but many people thought I was crazy. I told every person I knew that I was going to America. When these people asked how and when, I had no answer. As you can imagine, they all burst out laughing, but I was not offended. In fact I laughed with them, except I was laughing for a different reason. They laughed because they thought I was being funny and joking; I laughed because I meant what I said but could not get this through to them. At home, my parents were not laughing anymore. Instead, they were puzzled and annoyed. But no matter what reaction I got, I could not stop talking about going to America. I could see it in my spirit as clear as day, but I could not explain it. All I had to show was my words.

One morning, I woke up to go for an interview at a college about which I had found out from a cousin, Florence. This college prepared students for hospitality careers. Little did I know that God's soft voice had led me to apply there for a different reason.

The first question the admissions representative asked me after I introduced myself was, "Have you ever thought of studying in the

3

USA?" I nearly fell out of my chair. She said that she and the other admissions advisors had reviewed my application and had noticed that I already had two years of college in Kenya. They wondered if I might be interested in something different. Obviously, I told the woman yes—and the rest is history. That was the college that facilitated my coming to America. The process was long, but at last my parents believed me. They made big sacrifices to see my dream become a reality. Seeing as I come from a culture that discriminates against females, some people did not like it that my parents were trying to send a daughter, not a son, to the United States. However, many of these people eventually came on board and helped out financially. A year later I was in the USA, just like a dream.

My family, friends, and I still laugh about my American dream. I am still in awe of God's leading voice.

My Survival Mode

Beginning life on my own was tricky. I now laugh when looking back at some of my early experiences in the USA. The culture is very different. It took me some time to understand some of the differences in how people think and live. In Kenya, most people are very private and do not talk of personal things with strangers or with people who are not close family and trusted. In the USA, I first thought that everyone I came across and chatted with liked me a lot, because people talked to me about what I knew to be very personal things. I would meet someone at a bus stop and, during about half an hour of waiting, she would talk to me about the fights she had had with her boyfriend or husband, about going through divorce, about her husband having an affair, about her children being difficult and taking drugs, and the like. Many of these things were not things I was used to hearing, let alone from a total stranger. So I wondered what people trusted so much about me that they told me all the things they did.

My rude awakening came with my first job. A coworker at that time found me in the break room and shared with me some heartbreaking things that she was dealing with at home. I listened to her and supported her as best I could. I thought she deemed me to be a close friend. The very next morning, I met with her as I came to work and said hello to her. Not responding, she looked at me like it was the first time she had ever seen me. I was heartbroken and shocked. I wondered what could have happened. Only time taught me that it was a cultural difference that caused her to behave that way.

Another cultural difference between the USA and Kenya is the sense of personal responsibility (in the USA) and the sense of communal responsibility (in Kenya). As a young woman beginning life, I assumed that everyone around me understood I was struggling and was eager to help me out, like many older people will do in my native country. One day, I went for my first job orientation. I had only two dollars left after I paid bus fare to travel to the orientation site. One of the remaining dollars was for my fare home. During lunch, an older woman asked if I wanted to go for lunch with her. She offered to drive. Having been used to a culture wherein people tend to share with or give treats to younger people, I was super excited that this woman was so kind as to want to buy me lunch when I needed it most.

We went to a Taco Bell. I had no idea what happens in that place. I stopped to observe. As I did, the woman ordered her lunch, paid for it, and came back to find me in the line. She stated, "Once you find what you want to eat, pay for it there and find me at that table." I nearly fell over. What? I was in shock. *What do I do?* I thought. I had only one dollar to spare. I had to think quick and act quick.

The only thing I could get for less than a dollar was a soda. I went up and paid fifty cents for a soda, got my change, and joined my new friend. She asked if I wasn't hungry. Holding tight to my shock absorbers, I said I wasn't hungry. We spent lunchtime together, and then she drove me back to class. I had just learned another lesson.

On another day, I had to count coins that someone had given me to make bus fare. I counted a hundred cents and put them in a little plastic bag. When I got into the bus, I handed the bus driver my little bag of cents, letting him know it was a dollar. I will never forget the look in his eyes. He took the bag while staring at me. I was praying that he would accept my coins, because that was all the money I had. He put the bag of coins down and gave me a pass for my connection. I was happy. Once I went to a chair and turned to sit down, I noticed that the driver was still staring at me in amazement through the rearview mirror. It didn't matter to me what he was thinking. All I cared about was that he accepted my fare and gave me a pass for my next bus.

There are many other shocking examples of how I learned to function within a different culture. The lessons I learned were tough at the time, but by God's grace I learned them.

A Content Heart

"For I have learned to be content whatever the circumstances. I know what it is to be in need, and I know what it is to have plenty. I have learned the secret of being content in any and every situation, whether well fed or hungry, whether living in plenty or in want. I can do all this through him who gives me strength" (Philippians 4:11–13 NIV).

About seven months after I moved to the United States, I found an apartment and moved into it. Having left my parents' home in Kenya, I did not have any family to depend on. When I moved into my apartment, all I had was an air mattress, some blankets that were donated to me, and my clothes. It was in April, which was still very cold in Minnesota. I slept in five pairs of socks, five pairs of long pants, and at least three sweaters over my pajamas, because I was freezing at night. I had no idea what a thermostat was. The air mattress was made of plastic, which made matters worse. I did not know where to go to buy clothes; neither did I have the money to use for that. I did not know how to go anywhere other than to school, for which I took buses, and to church and work, to which I walked. My circumstances were difficult, although they did not seem that bad at the time. Having made a choice to be here, I was determined to make it, which kept me focused.

I was very excited to have an apartment for the first time in my life. Some of the people I worked with and went to school with wanted to see it. One woman I worked with requested to see my new place during a lunch break. She drove us there during our break. I opened the door, excited to welcome her in. As she took her first step in, her mouth dropped wide open. She walked across the room almost on her tiptoes, going into my bedroom. Her eyes were filling with tears as she walked back to where I was standing. I was surprised as I watched her. I did not understand what she had seen that shocked her so much. All of a sudden, she said through her tears, "You have nothing in your apartment!" This was the first time I realized I had nothing in my apartment, although I had been living in it for more than a month. At the corner of my bedroom lay a thin air mattress and some blankets—and that was all there was, other than my clothes in the closet. Yes, I had nothing up to this point, but I felt like I had everything I could have. My heart was content. God's peace and joy ruled my heart. What mattered was that I was in the USA, where I wanted to be. I was very thankful to God for the opportunity.

God had had a plan in urging this woman to come see my empty apartment that day. Her family, at completely no cost to me, changed my story. The next was my day to cry in shock. My coworker's family requested to have my keys while I was at work. After they came back to my office and had taken me to my apartment, I had to step back outside and look at my apartment number to make sure I was entering the right apartment. Inside I saw a set couch, a dining set, a microwave, a TV on a stand, plates, spoons, you name it. In my bedroom, I had a bed at last. It was made, and it looked beautiful. I sobbed as they waited patiently. They refused to take anything from me. It was one of the most humbling moments of my life. I will never forget that moment, with everything I felt. It seemed like a dream for a long time. My gratitude to God for that family will last forever.

During that same period of my life, I did not have a car; therefore, I walked to work and walked home. I walked during the freezing winters and even when I had night shifts. It never occurred to me that anyone would harm me. God is faithful, because no one attempted to. I took a bus to school because I was a full-time student. When I had evening classes, which ended at 10:00 p.m., I would transfer to a different bus in downtown Minneapolis at ten thirty or eleven. I heard gunshots several times as I waited for my bus at night. When this happened, I prayed and trusted God for my safety, and then I went to school again the next day because I felt that I had no choice but to tough it out. I didn't miss a single day of school or work because of fear. During winter, I would be so frozen that I hardly could move or speak when my bus arrived or by the time I got to my workplace. My first winter found me with zero winter clothes. What I wore were my clothes and jackets from Kenya, which is usually always hot, and usually above fifty degrees Fahrenheit when cold. I had no idea where or how to get appropriate clothing. I found out later that Goodwill sells used clothes very cheap. I focused on the reason I was in the United States, and I trusted God, who gave me the peace I cannot explain. He saw me through it all. I did not get sick during that time, and no harm came my way.

A friend of mine, Bernard, who became a brother at heart, left his car with me when he joined the Marines. He told me I could his car to learn to drive. He also left me close to two thousand dollars to make monthly payments until he could return for the car. I did not attempt to learn to drive until I was forced to, when I took another job to which I couldn't walk because the building was far away. Bernard's car had a manual transmission, so I got into some trouble while learning to drive with no one to teach me—well, no one other than a couple of friends who pointed out a few things about using a stick shift. One day, I tried to stop at a stoplight and didn't know how to balance the clutch yet. The car rolled back onto a police woman's car which got me into real trouble that day. I am very thankful to Bernard. Even though I had worn out the clutch of his car by the time he came back for the vehicle, he did not make me pay for it. In fact, he did not tell me what I had done until much later.

One of the major things that was very helpful to me psychologically was that before I left Kenya for the first time, I made a lot of inquiries. I inquired of as many people I could find who had lived in the United States what their experiences were. While some people gave me the wrong impression and talked about how wonderful life in the United States had been for them, some good friends gave me details of how tough it was for them. These latter people encouraged me and told me to be ready to do whatever work I could find in order to survive. These were people who studied in the United States and who are very successful in Kenya today. Some told me that they washed pots, cleaned bathrooms, washed people's houses and cars, etc., to survive. It was shocking to hear while looking at their successful lives, but it was still very motivating. Talking to these people prepared me by making me realize that it was not going to be easy. I felt better in that I was making an informed decision to continue my plans to go the United States. I became aware of the fact that I had to work very hard to make it and that I had to be ready to bear with whatever the circumstance, knowing that tough times don't have to last forever.

Divine Appointment

As a young woman growing up, I prayed many prayers to God, including prayers concerning the type of family I wished to have. My desire was to be stay-at-home mom while raising my children. As I got older, I imagined raising my own children more and more. I wanted to be extremely available and involved in their lives. I wanted them to know that they mattered to me more than anything else in the whole world. These were the deep longings of my heart among other things, like ministry to God's people. The desire to be a full-time mom while raising my children did not come to pass, but what God did grant me was the perfect way for dealing with what became my life circumstance. And He did this in the most amazing way.

I had finished a double major, a Bachelor of Arts in divinity and a Bachelor of Science in counseling psychology. I continued to work in the same facility I had been working in for about seven years while attending college. I was working on my Master of

Theological Studies. Many of my coworkers teased me for majoring in what they called "white-people fields." Many of them cared, and their intentions were good. Some felt bad for me and wanted to convince me to do what made sense. I understood where they were coming from, but they did not understand where I was coming from. I have had a calling for ministry in my heart since I was very young. I knew in my spirit that what I was doing in college was part of God's will for my life. I had a lot of peace and joy even though I did not find a job right after earning my bachelor's degree. People persuaded me to drop out of my MA program and to study nursing, a field with readily available job slots. I had a peace that I had known in other situations that eventually worked out. I knew beyond words that I was going to be okay. Yes, I am black with an African accent, living in the United States. In the natural, what my friends told me made perfect sense. But my heart would not change when I tried to reason with it.

My motivation was to start a charitable organization, the vision for which was in my heart. I did not know that this was going to happen much later in my life. God already had other plans worked out for that period of my life.

People all of a sudden started telling me about chaplain opportunities in nursing facilities and in hospitals. I remember thinking, *There is no way I will get a job as a chaplain,* as I am a young, black, short woman from Africa. In my mind, everything about me outwardly worked against me. Soon, someone else mentioned chaplain opportunities to me, wondering if being a chaplain was my goal. It wasn't. But I decided to check it out because of how much the idea was coming at me. I called a hospital, Hennepin County Medical Center (HCMC), in Minneapolis and left a voice mail message for the chaplain's department expressing my interest. I did not expect to hear back from them. I thought I was going to call a few more times. I was ready to call if I needed to. To my surprise, I received a call the very next day. The man who called me asked several questions about my faith background, education, etc. He stated after our conversation that he thought I should come in person and meet him and his coworker. Still wondering what I was thinking, and worrying that I was wasting my time, I went anyway and met them. They interviewed me and then said they thought I would make a good chaplain, but I needed to do my CPE (clinical pastoral education), which they informed me was a requirement. They gave me information on how to find CPE supervisors, which I pursued. I found many centers and prayerfully read about them as well as the supervisors. The first supervisor I called was the right one. He interviewed me over the phone and then set up a face-to-face interview. I made it through the interview process and was admitted to my first unit of CPE.

Being at the right place at the right time, with the right people, is the key for divine appointments. I just took steps of faith as God led me, even though nothing made sense to me yet. What I did not expect was that God had lined it up for me to meet a woman through this program. This meeting led to my choice of the chaplaincy as a career. In the past, chaplains were not required to have CPE. Many of the chaplains used to be retired pastors of various churches. That changed though. Some of those who were already chaplains without having undergone CPE were required to get it done now that the culture was changing.

The woman of whom I speak was a chaplain at Hospice of the Twin Cities. In about the second week of my interacting with her, she said that she was confident I would make a good chaplain. She recommended me for a casual position that was open at the Hospice of the Twin Cities. I remember thinking, *She must be out of her mind.* I had no experience. On top of that, I had other things working against me at that time. For example, I had never seen a black chaplain, let alone one with a Kenyan accent.

At first I started avoiding this woman because she kept asking if I had filled out an application. However, I could not avoid her enough, seeing as we had class together. I decided to fill out the application in order to get her off my back. I did not have any faith in myself at that time, but God remained faithful. The day after I had submitted my application, I received a call and was scheduled for an interview. I still did not believe it, but I was glad my new friend would not admonish me again for not applying for the job. So I went for the interview.

It was my first professional interview, and it was a long one. I thought that it was a good and interesting experience. I received another call and was scheduled for a second interview. I still had no faith that I would actually get the job, but I kept moving forward, in obedience to the process. In another two days, I received a call with a job offer. I still remember exactly where I was standing in my apartment when I answered that phone call. I could not believe that this was happening. But it was real. I was not even done with my CPE and was still working on my master's program. The company held the position for me for two months, until I was done with my CPE and could start working with them. Shortly after that, I finished my master's program as well. I did not go seeking for a different job at that point. I am thankful I listened to the impressions of my heart. I believe this job was brought my way for Nate's sake.

The ten years I worked for Hospice of the Twin Cities were the most difficult years of my life, yet during that time I was present for my son in a way that I would never have imagined I could be, especially as a single mother. Nate's school schedule worked out perfectly in the first eight years. I was able to drop him at school and then be at work in time for meetings. Other than the fact that my position was generally flexible with regard to scheduling, the company cared for its employees in a very personal way. As a result, people cared about each other and for the patients whom we served. Our work environment was one to be envied. I also believe I was divinely watched over, because not everyone I worked with understood what I was living through on a daily basis. I was very proud to be part of a company that was named as one of the top hundred best work places in Minnesota, by star tribune in 2012. I can testify that the organization was appropriately named as such.

As far as I am concerned, the fact that I had gotten this job could not have been a coincidence. I believed that God worked it all out. I believe that this was how God had answered my prayers, including the one about my desire to be able to raise my children closely at a time when it would have been impossible in the natural. What is more mind-blowing to me is that I did not look for a job, and in fact had felt no desire to look for a job, after finishing my two bachelor's degrees. I thank God that He gave me the peace just to be still and wait on Him. While I was going through college, I had no idea how God was going to make things work out for me, but I had much peace in knowing that I was going to be okay. In His perfect time and in His own way, He has a way of making all things beautiful for the glory of His name. He knew I needed to work for such a company before I knew that Hospice of the Twin Cities existed. Given my son's medical journey, I totally believe I would have been fired many times from most other workplaces. I held this position for ten years. I was blessed beyond expression by this company and the people I worked with. I believe this position came to my life as part of God's faithfulness toward Nate's life.

As a Single Mother

Born and raised in a village in Meru, Kenya, I did not know any single mother while I was growing up. The few young girls who had gotten pregnant were part of families, and their children were raised within the family. Divorce was news I heard of, but it did not make any sense in my reality. The first time I heard that someone whom I knew from a distance was going through divorce was in my high school years. In my boarding school life, I knew a couple of kids who said their parents were divorced, but they didn't talk much about it. In cases of death of a father or of a mother of young children, families were very involved. Children were raised by the family, including the extended family. But none of these things prepared me for my divorce or for single motherhood. Neither did anything prepare me for the shocks delivered by my stepfamily years later, when I was maltreated, judged, hated, and schemed against just for being remarried.

I became a single mother in a foreign country when my son was two and half years old. I was completely devastated, but I approached my task with courage, because I knew it was a better choice for my child than was the situation I had been in prior to becoming a single mother. Some of the most important values I held were shattered at the time of my divorce. I had desired to raise a family like my mom and dad had done. I wanted to have many children of one biological father and raise them with him, watch them play, listen to them scream with joy, see them go to school, and watch them grow into adults, just as my parents had experienced when they raised me. I had to accept that my many beautiful dreams of life would never become a reality after I was divorced. I had to make a choice to be bitter or better. I had other dreams I still could see coming to pass, depending on who God made me to be. I had a child whose future would most probably depend on every choice I made. Having my son and feeling responsible for his life gave me strength and the will to let go of what had become of my life and to focus on giving him the best that I could. I wanted him to know unconditional love, peace, and joy. I wanted him to know that he was worth having a parent who was committed to him. I wanted him to grow up knowing that he was not to blame for the parting of ways of his parents and that he had no single part to play in it. I wanted him to believe in himself and to become all what God had purposed him to be. So I reoriented my heart and mind on how I had been raised. Although I was alone now, I could take some lessons from my two parents as well as learn from other sources around me.

When I was growing up, there was no hitting, no name-calling, no shaming, and no being put down. We had a peaceful home atmosphere, and we all got along. We children were protected. I did not have exposure to abuse except for when people came to ask my parents for help and I heard their stories. Starting life on my own, which unfortunately was during a time when I was far away from my family, was very difficult. The experiences I had from the moment I came to America were very different from those I had had when I lived with a family that always provided for me and protected me. Being a single mother was only an additional responsibility. I not only had my issues to sort out, but I also had a child to worry about.

The hardest thing I have had to do has been advocating for my children. The world has a tendency to classify everyone in groups and treat each person as a number or a case within different systems. No one likes to be classified or to be treated as a number, but we tend to have no problem doing this to each other. The systems think in terms of their interests and profits, not in terms of what is right and just. Nothing in my upbringing prepared me for this, except that my parents gave me a strong backbone when it comes to who I am in God.

The greatest thing I am thankful for is that my parents raised me and my siblings in faith. It was practiced and emphasized in our home that God was all one ever needed to get through life. We prayed about everything and gave thanks to God for everything. We prayed before going to bed and at the start of each day. My parents encouraged us children to believe in ourselves and never to give up. They built us up and made it very clear to us that we mattered to them. The impact my parents had on my life became evident to me when I found myself alone with a child to raise. It did not take me long to realize that my son was my responsibility. I didn't have time to mourn over my losses at his expense. I prayed for God's grace and guidance, picked myself up, and with God's help faced life head-on.

What Worked

I believe that children adjust as well as the adults in their lives do. I kept this fact in mind as I went through my separation and divorce. I made up my mind that my child deserved a committed mother, which helped me keep my feelings in check. Staying calm and encouraging communication with Nathanael helped a great deal. I intentionally kept my mood positive for his sake. I kept reminding him that both of his parents loved him and that it was not his fault we were now living separately. I was intentional about making the best of my bad situation for my son's sake. I read the book of Proverbs a lot during this time, searching for the voice of God in it. I find that the book of Proverbs states facts about life and is simple. Every action has a reaction, for example. Being aware of what I wanted for my children helped me tremendously. I not only prayed about what I wanted for my children, but I also made appropriate efforts in that direction.

I believe that a person can only give what she has. If I was not taking care of myself, then I could not take care of my child appropriately. To be a good mother, I made a choice to clean up my inner person. I accepted my anger and frustration with life, and then I sought out counseling services as well as mature believers to help me heal. I was accountable to the people I trusted by sharing how I was feeling and what I was dealing with day by day. Staying aware of my feelings about and my struggles with separation and divorce, as well as seeking support, helped me stay calm for my son. It also helped me hold life together.

Another major thing I keep in mind as a parent is what kind of people I would like my children to grow up to be. This helps me make simple, day-to-day decisions about how I deal with my children. It helps me stay purposeful with parenting and keeps me from flowing with my feelings. For example, disciplining my child has never been fun to me. Yet if I don't discipline them, the cruel world will do it the hard way. I love my children. As much as is possible, I would like them to be loved and accepted by others. I realize this will not happen just because they are my children and I want it to happen. I therefore love them enough to raise them for the world. I train them to respect authority, and this starts with me as the parent. I start with parenting as soon as my child is born. I don't believe in waiting until children are older to parent them. I love to build them up and teach them what the Word of God says about their existence. I like them to know they are at the top of my priorities because they are very special to me. Yet I like them to know that other people's children are very special to their parents too and that we must be respectful of everyone. I don't entertain any cute behaviors of today that I know will cause a problem tomorrow. I don't want my children to think they can have everything they want or demand, because this will cause them pain in the future. I don't want them to grow up thinking they can have their way in everything, because that is not true. As a parent, because I don't believe it is in the best interests of my children to do whatever they want whenever they want to do, I don't allow them to have TVs or computers in their bedrooms. Neither do my children spend as much time as they wish in front of the screen. My goal is to raise them to become productive in the future and to be able to function in the tough world.

God's grace was upon my life when I became a single mother. I saw His manifestation. For many years before I became a mother, I prayed very specific prayers concerning what I desired for my children. When I was divorced, I prayed that it would not affect my son's life in a major way. I planned for that as much as I could by asking for help from my family. I wanted to keep my son's life as stable as I could and to keep him loved through the tough process of separation and divorce. I didn't know how possible some of my desires would be, given how much my life was changing. However, I was left amazed by how faithful God is even when circumstances seem impossible in the natural. At the time of my separation, God divinely opened a door for me to take a position as a chaplain, a job that paid me well and gave me a more flexible schedule. I also had specifically prayed that my children would be raised within their home until they came to be of school age. God also opened the door for my mother to come to the United States from Kenya to help me with my son. God answered my prayers in spite of my circumstances. Nathanael was raised in his home with the help of his grandma until he was about four and half years old. After my mother went back to Kenya, Nathanael received care at home or in the homes of my longtime friends Agnes and Alice, where he had their children as friends. These friends' children, who grew up around Nathanael, thankfully also provided him with a sort of brotherhood. When he turned five years old, he started full-day kindergarten at LoveWorks Academy. I took him to school in the morning and picked him up in the afternoon. I was then usually home with him for the rest of the day.

The fact that my son had a complicated medical condition topped off my single motherhood. Nathanael was in the hospital on a regular basis. Hospitals became a second home to us. He would be hospitalized a month at a time, or for a week, or for several days—and this happened over and over. Almost all of the staff members working different shifts knew us in the hospitals to which he was most regularly admitted. We were also very frequent visitors to the ERs when he was not hospitalized. We were often in radiology departments to have scans of his brain done whenever he was throwing up or having headaches, which happened regularly. I was constantly on the run, trying to keep life together. I learned to surrender to God, because there was nothing left for me to do. My son was my first priority. I wanted to be with him when he was in the hospitals, and I *was* with him each and every time. I had seen a nurse try to mistreat my son once, and I could not live with the thought of this happening to him without anyone there to stand up for him. That meant that I was absent a lot from work. Many times I was called while I was work to pick up Nate from school or from home and take him to the hospital or deal with him when he started having seizures. I surrendered my job to God and trusted that He would always provide Nathanael and me with what we needed to survive. I had once slept on a floor when I moved to the United States; I found out that the lowest a person can go down is into the ground, which holds a dead body firmly. In a sense, this fact kept me peaceful. What mattered to me was being present for my son during his suffering. That was what mattered most to my son as well. I put everything I could toward doing my job when things were okay at home. Many times I did the tasks that I could do beside my son's hospital bed in order to avoid being called out for not doing my work. There were many times when I felt like I was crumpling down into a pile, but I kept my mind focused on the fact that I was doing what I was doing for my son. I never complained. If anything, I was thankful that I could get some work done by his bedside and manage to keep my job under the circumstances. When the hospital found a volunteer to sit with my son during the times when I had no help, I hurried home to take a shower and then came back to the hospital. It all worked out; my son never spent a single day in the hospital without me being by his side. And that had been my prayer. Although life is hard and I had to make sacrifices, God knows no impossibilities when you ask things according to His will.

Financially, I basically lived by faith. I was not broke because I was lazy or was having too much fun in life. So I never let myself worry about what we did not have and how we were going to survive. I had a knowing in my heart that it was going to be okay each time, and it was okay. I prayed and kept being present for my son as my top priority. I trusted God to see us through. Even though I had a job that paid me reasonably well, I was not paid for the times when I was away from work on account of my son's being sick. I was paid hourly. If I did not work, I did not get paid. I never accumulated sick time because I took more sick days than I accumulated, of course. I bounced from hospital to work, back and forth. Other than our two trips to Kenya, I did not take my son for a vacation away. I didn't even think about it. But we did do fun things. I found many cheap or free places where I could take my son for fun. I kept my mind focused on giving him the happiest childhood I could afford. He played and lived a normal life when he was not in the hospital. But one day, after a while of not being hospitalized, Nate asked me when he was going to be hospitalized again. That surprised me, so I asked him why he had asked that, only to find out that his interpretation of vacation was time away from home, which to him meant being in the hospital. (He was then in school and getting all sorts of ideas from the other kids.) That made me very sad. I remember crying hard to God that night. I took whatever little money I had and that weekend drove to Duluth with Nate. We stayed in a hotel for two nights and went sightseeing during the day. I talked to him about what vacation meant then. I will never forget that experience. For the first time, he had a vacation where he was not poked with needles and didn't have IV tubes hooked to his arms or oxygen meters tied to his toes. From that time on, I made it my goal to get Nathanael to a hotel for a night or two when I could—and he no longer wanted to be hospitalized for his vacations. Other than that, I lived a very simple life. We found a lot of happiness in spending time together and in doing or seeing the simple things of life. God came through each time in different ways. We were never kicked out of the apartment for not paying rent; neither did we go to bed hungry for a single day. Sometimes friends got together and surprised me with a gift of unexpected money to pay my bills.

God often surprised me, each time in a different way. At the hospital, I used the meal tickets given to those with less income and long hospital stays in order to survive. Faithful friends Agnes, Alice, and Jennifer, among others, brought me food to the hospital without getting tired of it. My bosses and many of my coworkers remained supportive of me during times when I did not expect them to. I was never fired or disciplined for my numerous absences.

I can truly say that God is faithful, because there was no other way I would have made it through those circumstances.

I bought books about raising a boy and read them, which shed a lot of light on how boys think and what boys need. One of the things I came to terms with was that I could be a great mother to my son, but I could not provide the male-specific things that every child needs (although not every child gets it). This was devastating at first, but as I prayed God gave me peace and ideas. Were it not for reading, I most probably would have been raising my son with unrealistic expectations of him as a boy. For support, I had my childhood neighbor Duncan, who ended up being my neighbor in the United States at that time, and my cousin Eric, who lived in the area. I intentionally sought out these healthy relationships so that my son would have some males around him on a regular basis. Uncle Duncan was a next door neighbor who gave Nate a lot of love and support, including during the many times when Nate was in the hospital. Uncle Eric had a drive to make if he wanted to see us, but he made a point to come around as often as he could. My dad also came to help support Nate for an extended period while Nate was sick, but Dad also wanted to provide that male aspect in his grandson's life. Nathanael always looked forward to his time together with Uncle Duncan or Uncle Eric, and he loved every minute of the time spent with his grandpa in the United States and when we visited Kenya. Another person who made a huge difference in Nate's life was his godfather, Mac. I still remember little Nate sitting on Mac's lap. The more I watched my son with these men, the more it made sense to me why, as a mother and a woman, I couldn't give him what they were giving him. I will forever be thankful for these relationships, because they filled the gap in Nathanael's life that I would never have been able to fill.

By the time my son started school, God had already made a way where there otherwise would have been no way. I had asked God to make a way for me to take my children to school and then pick them up after school every day. In addition to the fact that Nathanael's medical condition made him delicate, I had a desire to provide transportation for my children. Although I was a single mother with a lot of life crises, God was not limited to the crises of my life. He provided my job position long before Nathanael went to school. At the time when Nathanael started school, his schedule matched my work schedule. I made it happen as a single mother to take my son to school and pick him up as I had prayed. I have come to believe in the truth of the saying "Where there is a will there is a way." The way may not always come easy, but being specific about what you want is very helpful in getting what you want. With God's help, I found trusted people who came to my home to babysit my children, because that was what I wanted and sought after. I made a huge financial sacrifice to have this happen, but it was well worth it. I believe in protecting my children's emotional development as much as I possibly can as well as providing as much stability as possible throughout their growing years, especially during the initial five years of their lives. I prefer that they stay in their home, because I can't control other people's environments. I can, on the other hand, control my own environment. I can choose what I want to have around my children. Being in their home while young enabled my children to sleep as much as they needed to in the mornings, which I believe is very important.

The hardest thing I have had to do, something that I couldn't avoid, is advocate for my children. The most important thing for me to remember is that the battles I face belong to God as long as I stand for what is true. Sometimes standing for what is right means more suffering. What I have learned to look for is God's provision, which may lead me in a different direction so that I don't have to be concerned about the former situations. For example, when I have encountered a person who misuse power to exalt their selfish interests against my child or myself; I don't seek to win in such situations. Instead, I seek God to learn what each attack means for me or for my child. I believe that all things work for good for they who trust in God and are called according to His purpose, even when there is pain and suffering. The world's systems and many people put their interests before justice, which makes life very difficult. I have had to say no when there was need to say no, which does not always make things easy. In Acts 16, Paul and Silas set a demon-possessed slave girl free. This girl's masters did not rejoice that she was set free from demonic possession. Instead, they got mad because they were not going to be able to use her to make money any longer. As a result, Paul and Silas were beat up and put into jail, all because these masters, who were rich and powerful, were more concerned about their profits than with the well-being of the slave girl. Paul and Silas trusted God even in their suffering for doing good. In our world today, many people have died fighting for justice and freedom. Such things remind me that my situations aren't unique. There is really no way to defend oneself against such things other than to depend on God.

I have been at hospitals a lot, and it has not always been easy. Dealing with schools has been the worst of my child's experiences as well as mine, although some of the school experiences have been excellent. Sometimes, I have been faced with two choices: turn and run away, or face the issue and stand for what I believe to be in my child's best interests. Many people tend to listen and agree to work things out after I speak up for my child. Working within the system, people who work with the right heart may not notice a struggle until you point it out, because they have other people and issues they are working on. That is usually my first assumption. Many people have found solutions and have helped out, not making a big deal of the fact that I asked for assistance or pointed out a need that had been overlooked. Some of these people have said to me that more parents need to advocate for their children. Other people have met me with resistance because I have made their work more difficult by asking for help. A few have become pumped up with pride right away, determined to prove that their decision is final, because that is their territory and because you, by voicing a concern, questioned their power. No matter what the situation, I have realized, when raising a child with any complications, that it is extremely difficult and not everyone cares the same way. While many people enter various professions for the right reasons, there is a group of people in every profession who are in it for the wrong reasons. I find nothing wrong with advocating for my children. In fact, I believe there is everything wrong with not advocating for them when there is a need to. Fortunately, although I have had some very bad experiences with advocacy, I have been showered with blessings in the process. I have come to learn that there are many good and kindhearted people around me who are willing to help and to make life better for others.

Hard work pays. I learned this from my parents. They worked very hard and taught us children to work hard as we were growing up. I knew I had to make many sacrifices if I wanted to give my children the life I dreamt of giving them. Proverbs 10:4 could not make it any clearer to me: "Lazy people are soon poor; hard workers get rich." I am a believer in hard work. I do not sit around and hold a pity party for myself. I did not go after the social security benefits to which my son was entitled because of his medical condition. People said that quitting my job would have qualified us for those benefits, but instead I chose to work. It was not easy to hold onto a spiritually, emotionally, and mentally demanding career for ten years given my circumstances, but God saw me through. And I did not leave that job until I clearly knew it was time for me to leave. When I held my position at Hospice of the Twin Cities, I worked from wherever I was in order to get the job done. There were many times when I worked from the hospital when my son was an inpatient. At midnight I would be awake, so I worked on my laptop after my son fell asleep and the hospital activities calmed down. No one needed to know where I was working from. All that mattered was that I got my job done. I never complained of being tired or having to work the way I did. I was extremely thankful, always, that I had a job. I talked with some people who were fired after they took a few days off to tend to a sick child, so I never took my job for granted. Employers don't fire people because they don't care. I believe they feel bad when they fire someone. But if all employers kept all of their workers because they would feel bad firing them, then all companies would close down. Still, I do believe there are many employers who are unreasonable and who don't value their employees. But for those who care, they still have work to be done, no matter how much they may value their employees. I talked very little about my life struggles at work. I never came to work talking about how I had to work from the hospital. I did not want to overwhelm my company into firing me. So I kept my struggles to myself and just worked with a lot of gratitude. Part of the time when I was a single mother, I was also a student. I chose not to quit. I did my schoolwork from wherever I was, too. I kept the hope in my heart that tough circumstances do not last forever. I was determined to see the other end of my struggles.

To finish up at my school, I sometimes took my son to class with me. I was attending evening classes, from 6:00 p.m. to 10:00 p.m. once a week. For a short period, my mother had gone back to Kenya. What I did was talk to my four- or five-year old son before class about my expectations of him while I attended class. I did it every time I took him with me, and it worked every time. I brought his coloring books, picture books, and pencils and pens. I talked to my professors about my life situation, and they were very understanding. More so, things worked out because my son did not cause any problem in class on any of the days I brought him with me. When he got tired, I laid out his mat on the floor at the back of the room, which was where I sat with him. He slept until class was over. One major thing I have found that works well is to talk about my expectations to my children before we leave the house. I have not had to deal with temper tantrums from my children. I believe this is because I practice laying down my expectations before the kids lay their own in their minds. I also learned to ask others for understanding when I believed in God for something. For example, when bringing my child to class, I chose to ask my professors for what I needed instead of quitting school. I have realized that what Jesus said in Mark 11:24 (NASB) is true for me: "Therefore I say to you, all things for which you pray and ask, believe that you have received them, and they will be granted you." Many people have been willing to work with me when I have directly asked for what I needed. I am not afraid to ask anymore, because the worst I can get is no for an answer. I am okay with no. When I get a no, I don't quit; I ask God where I should go next. I keep my attitude toward life positive, and it works for me.

Concerning my children directly, my goal is to raise them in the best way possible. One of my favorite things to do is to hold my babies in my arms as much as I possibly can. My babies are my gifts from God. My biggest reason for holding my babies is because they need to be held. Holding and cradling a baby is one of the bests gifts you can give to a child, and it is one that is free of charge. I believe it provides a sense of security, affection, and connection. I believe that I have very few years in which to hold my babies in my arms, yet doing so makes such a huge difference in who they become as older people. When they are babies, I hold them at every opportunity, but I keep in mind that I must give them time to develop in their independence as well. Although this is not the reason I hold my babies, I must admit that it is one of the greatest feelings to me as a mother, one that brings me such a sense awe for God. As they get older and start to move around and play, I wait for the times when they come running to my lap. I like to communicate to them how special they are to me. I tell them that I am available to them when they need me.

Other than making eye contact with my children and talking to them about how much they mean to me, I love reading to them the Bible stories and Scriptures about who God is, what faith means, and how much He loves them. I believe we are spirit beings. The sooner a child is introduced to anything, the higher the chances are that it will stick with them. I believe that my children hear and understand what I read to them deep in their spirits. I believe God's Spirit is alive in my little babies and working within them. When they were younger, I read to them fun kids' stories. As they got older, I played did book-related games with them, especially Nate. I also made up songs in gratitude for them as well as worship songs. Because time goes so fast and children grow up so quickly, investing time in my children is my highest ministry while my children are young. I train them to embrace simply being who God made them to be. I teach them to be still, peaceful, quiet, and calm in a world that moves fast even when there is no reason to be in a hurry.

I believe children should be given a chance to be children. I am okay with the fact that my own kids make messes. My home is 100 percent their home. They are not afraid or wondering what to expect at any time. They are free to play, talk, ask questions, etc. I believe that rules should be made by a parent or parents. I communicate my house rules to my children, providing them with age-appropriate reasons for each of the rules. I believe that helping my children understand why there are rules, instead of imposing rules on them, helps them to take ownership of the rules. I have found this method to work.

When my children were younger, I took them to the mall, the zoo, parks, and the like. These places did not cost me much, if anything, but my children enjoyed them. I found out there are many simple things to do with a child and simultaneously provide playmates if you are looking. Things that I have always been less lenient about when raising my children include TV time, computer time, and time with most electronic gadgets. My children's screen time is very limited because I do not believe in screen training. I believe in children using their creativity, and that is what I encourage. As far as nutrition is concerned, I love to cook. Nate did not eat fast foods until he went to kindergarten. Both of my children ate vegetables growing up, and today none of my children has a problem with eating any vegetables. Eating out is an occasional thing, and getting fast food is a rare experience. I do not like having more health problems to deal with than I need to, and I believe that what we eat in a sense makes us. I do not just feed my children vegetables; I also eat veggies, and that makes it normal for them. It is healthier, it is cheaper, and it works. Both Nathanael and Sally have very rarely gone to a doctor's office other than for Nathanael's annual checkups for his brain-related problems. I believe that what we feed our bodies has a huge impact on our health.

Personal responsibility is something I believe in. I trained Nate to start taking responsibility from an early age. While it might be a lot of fun to do things for our children, it isn't in their best interests, I believe. I started to teach Nate to do things for himself as I felt he was capable. I taught him boundaries, too. My children know I am their parent and they are my children—and there is no equal friendship between us. Especially as a single mother with a son, I was very adamant about never needing my son emotionally. I was intentional in that whatever I did in connection to him was done for his benefit, not mine. Parents set home rules and children follow home rules. My children don't do whatever they want to do in my home. They do only what they are allowed to do, for the periods it is allowed. I believe love comes with discipline, so I was never afraid to hurt Nate's feelings when he needed discipline. I encouraged him to verbalize his feelings and kept that going. I talked (and I still do) to him about expectations ahead of time, and that has been very helpful. I invested my time in explaining things clearly to him so that he was not just obeying me but also understood why, to make it his choice. I raised him as intentionally as I possibly could. Later, this made things easier for Sally, because Nathanael sets such a great example for her.

When Steve, my husband, met my son, he never hesitated to be part of his life, in spite of the complications involved. And the moment he held little Sally in his arms, he never wanted to let go. My son did not fight me about having someone else in my life and getting remarried. He knew what his place was very securely and without any confusion, and I was happy for that. But it took work and intention, and God's help. Being that my son needed extra attention on account of his medical condition, I made an intentional decision to give my daughter a lot of attention so that she did not grow up feeling like she was less important. I did not want her to feel left out at a young age because there was no way of making her understand the circumstances. I was often forced to drop everything and to run to her brother. Being aware of what that could mean to my daughter was very helpful.

My encouragement to single parents is to do your part diligently and to watch God do His part. I believe many times that God wants to bless our lives but that we are not ready when our blessings show up, so they leave. I have met people who had relationships that started out beautifully but that ultimately did not work out because the children were not trained to know what their position was. Children should always be children and parents should always be parents, whether in two-parent families or single-parent families. The moment those roles are misunderstood, the future of many relationships is in jeopardy. The party responsible for defining these roles is the parent, not the child.

I believe you can do anything you put your mind to. We have more potential than we put into use.

I Made a Choice

There I was divorced and with a child, pregnant out of wedlock, and abandoned. I felt distressed, angry, ashamed, rejected, and any other feeling associates with being betrayed. I held myself together for my son's sake when I was around him, because I knew it was the right thing to do. As soon as he went to bed each night, I, for a period of time, would cry myself to sleep. I never missed a day of work as a chaplain proving spiritual care and emotional support for our patients and their families. However, it took a lot of energy to cover up the shame I carried with me day after day. One Saturday morning as I was cleaning up my apartment, I came across a book that caught my eye. I picked up the book and started going through it. This book was about spiritual things that affect unborn babies in ways that could change the rest of their lives. That caught my attention. As I read the book, I was surprised and at the same time very grateful. I believe God led me to that book to save my unborn baby, Sally, from the emotional struggles I was dealing with. It brought to my attention that unborn babies can sense their mother's emotions. It said that a mother suffering shame can pass the shame to the baby inside her so that the child is born and lives with feelings of shame without understanding why. The same would be true for all the emotions that a pregnant mother might have. God spoke to me through that book. It was like a slap on my face. Instantly, I decided my unborn child was more important than all the negative feelings I had been carrying. Thankfully, I was early in my pregnancy.

I made up my mind that, moving forward, I was not going to let my child suffer things that she did not ask for. I immediately let go of all the negative emotions I was feeling and decided to give her what she deserved: peace! I started confessing God's Word and making positive statements out loud to my baby, as well as intentionally thinking positive thoughts. The fact is, I always wanted more children and I was not sad that I was pregnant. I was sad about my circumstances. I had never for one moment of my life thought that I would be pregnant and abandoned by the father of my child, let alone endure the other difficulties of my life. I decided to focus on what was important to me, which was the fact that I had been trusting God for more children in my life and I was pregnant.

When I was about two months pregnant, my gynecologist ordered an ultrasound. It was then that I was informed I was having a baby girl. This would be confirmed at five months. There is power in intentional decisions. The moment I made up my mind about how I wanted life to proceed, I stopped crying and started celebrating my daughter. When my pregnancy was finally visible, some people thought I didn't care that I was divorced and now pregnant with no husband. The fact is I cared a lot but not in the way they thought I should. In another sense they were right, because I had made up my mind not to care about what people were going to think or say. Many things were said to me, especially by my fellow believers in Jesus Christ. I could not win the battle of people's judgment and condemnation of me. The only battle I could win was the one of protecting my daughter—and I was determined to win it.

The moment I had been informed that this child was a girl, I went home and found possible names for my daughter. I believe there is power in a parent's naming his or her child. I name my children based on my prayers for their lives, like my parents taught me to do. For that reason, I wanted names that would bode well for my daughter's entire life, names that would bring blessings and erase any negativity that comes with the confessions of others. I prayed for Sally by using her name, and every time I talked about her, I called her by her name, which I believe to be a confession of her destiny.

The voice of God, through a simple book, led me to live differently than I would have under the circumstances. For example, I didn't shy away from going to church, which would have been difficult to do on my own because I have a fear of people. I was also thankful that my son, who is always ready for church every Sunday, did not have to miss church on account of his mom's choices.

The most difficult thing I needed to do, I felt, was to face my pastor, Randy, whom I respect and who has been supportive of my spiritual journey. I felt I owed it to him to tell him that I was pregnant. I had asked God to forgive me, and I believed He did according to His Word. That did not make it easier to face my pastor, as I was afraid of what his response would be. I was afraid he would take away my ordination and have nothing else to do with me. I went to God and prayed about it, and God gave me peace. When I surrendered to God, fear left me. I was all of a sudden ready for whatever decision Pastor Randy would make. I felt he had a right to do whatever he chose to do. I made up my mind that I would be okay with his decision and not be offended, no matter what decision he made. At that moment, I chose to do what I knew to do: leave every outcome to God.

When the day for me to speak to Pastor Randy finally came, I sat in his meeting room with him. Before I said why I was there, he stated, "You are pregnant, aren't you?" That was so helpful, because those were the hardest words for me to say at that time. I said yes. I saw the pain on his face, pain that I would expect to see from a caring father. Tears were going down my face for lack of words. To my surprise, I did not sense judgment from him. What I sensed coming from him was genuine care. He was heartbroken about my circumstances, like my own father was. He sat with me, listened to me, and did not condemn me. He encouraged me to forgive myself as God forgave me and to do what was right as I moved forward. He encouraged me not to let shame keep me away from the love of God. He also encouraged me to continue attending church. Because I felt accepted by my pastor, it did not matter how many other people might reject me and look down on me. I went to church every Sunday without fail. God can use one person to make such a difference when we need it most, and in my church He used my pastor.

By the time I started looking pregnant, I had come to peace with myself before God and with those who cared about me as a person. Many others people passed judgment against me and passed rumors that I never had any idea where their version of stories came from. None of the gossiping people ever asked me what had happened or showed any concern. I did not allow those things to affect me negatively though. This period of my life turned out to be such a learning experience about people in general, especially my fellow Christians. Some believers were not happy that I went to church in my pregnant state. They made this clear to me by how they treated me at church. Some repeated their behavior every time they saw me or had a chance. I was surprised that I was very ill-treated by church people whom I knew from various congregations while I received a lot of grace, kindness, and support at my workplace. I would have expected it to be the other way round, based on God's Word, specifically Galatians 6:1–2: "Brothers, if anyone is caught in any transgression, you who are spiritual should restore him in a spirit of gentleness. Keep watch on yourself, lest you too be tempted. Bear one another's burdens, and so fulfill the law of Christ." Instead I experienced what some unknown author wrote: "Christians are the only army in the world who kill their own wounded."

I received support from my family, a few of my close friends, my pastor, and my coworkers. I learned never to take grace for granted in my life. I refused to let any of the negativity control me. I needed the one voice of God speaking to me and guiding me, and I knew beyond a doubt that I had that. I also focused on what was important to me, which was the best interests of my children. I chose not to get upset at anyone's opinion of me, as everyone is entitled to have an opinion. I opened my eyes to learning, and I focused on staying healthy. Through it all, I became stronger and better. Eventually everything worked out for my good.

My Father's Blessing

When I found out I was pregnant out of wedlock, I, rejected and abandoned, was devastated. I was an ordained minister who preached to people on many occasions in different places to which I was invited. Many people did not judge me for having been divorced. My announcing that I was pregnant and alone did it though. Many people did not look at me the same way after that. The people who judged me the most didn't ever ask me what my story was. I was given a death sentence. I was shunned and labeled, which should not have surprised me. No matter what the situation is, culturally the woman is to blame when she turns up pregnant and without a partner. The man is not mentioned because he is a man. Thankfully, I had found out that I was pregnant during a time when my father had come from Kenya to help me with my son. I had to break the news to my father as well, and that was really hard.

People's reactions were hard for me to take, but they were not as piercing as my dad's initial words. First, he nearly passed out, which I expected. I watched him go through the cycle of shock. I was not sure that he had heard me correctly, so I repeated my words. After a while, he said sadly, "You will never find anyone to marry you, for sure." He was not being mean at all. That was his cultural training speaking through him. He was in a lot of pain when he said those words. I felt as if a sharp knife had gone through my chest, all the way through to my back. That was the end of our conversation for that moment. I was hurt but did not want to show my father what his words had done to me. I excused myself and went to my bedroom. In my solitude, I sobbed. Later that day, my father inquired more about my situation and asked who was responsible for my pregnancy, because he wanted to know who had done this to his daughter. Even though he had met the man who had fathered sally, I did not find it necessary to tell my dad his name, because it was not going to make things better. I will never forget the pain on my father's face. But he was able to swallow the bullet and thereafter to support me in the way he knew best. He let me know that my family would always be there for me and my children. He promised me that he and my mom were going to give me a piece of their land to help me out. I did not want to hear any of his sympathetic statements, but I listened politely as those initial words played over and over in my mind. On the inside I was screaming in anguish. That night, I went before God and cried to Him again. I was so hurt, I could not stop crying. I did not know how to handle my father's words. I believe that a parent's words can be very powerful. I did not want my father to believe the worst about me. I wanted him still to believe in me. God heard my cry and comforted me as well as showed me exactly how to approach my father about my pregnancy.

The next morning after breakfast, I stood before my father with a bottle of anointing oil. My father is Catholic and had never handled anointing oil in his entire life. I asked him to pray for me and anoint me with oil. I coached him a little bit on how to use the oil. He was in surprise and confusion, but I did not pay attention to that. I knew I could not ask my father to take back his words, so I requested very specific prayers from him. I requested him to pray to God for my protection and the protection of my children. I requested him to pray that God give me a husband and my children a dad. I requested that he pray for my prosperity. With those words, I took my knee. Dad paused for a moment, but my head was bowed on my knees and I did not look up. The next thing I felt was his index finger with the anointing oil on my forehead. He prayed for me in the name of the Father and the Son and the Holy Spirit, exactly as I had requested. My son, Nathanael, was able to capture a photo of me at that moment. I will cherish that photo forever. When my dad was done anointing me, I asked him to pray for my son, to ask that God bring a dad into Nate's life along with the daughter inside me. My son went to his knees, and his grandpa prayed for him without hesitation. Once my dad was done, I, in heartfelt humility, said to him, "Daddy, from now on we will believe God for what you have just prayed for us. We won't believe our culture, right, Dad?" He nodded his head and said yes, and I could tell he was moved. Nathanael was stable by then. Not long after that, my father returned to his home in Kenya.

Blessings of a parent are powerful. Six months from the time of my father's prayers, which was three months after my daughter was born, I met my husband Steve. I am so glad I did not settle for the hurt. I love my dad, and I knew that he would never do anything to hurt me. But if I had let that day go by and had done nothing about it, then our relationship might have changed for the worse, leaving him and me more hurt. Instead, the voice of God led to blessings, giving me a moment with my father that I will cherish for the rest of my life. I received his blessing on my life when I really needed it.

Divine Interventions

One particular summer morning began like any other ordinary day. Nate was out of school for summer. I had dropped him at a friend's house for day care while I went to work. It was exactly two weeks from the day Nate had had a medical emergency and had quit breathing, a very traumatic event. After that time, I started noticing pain all over my body. I felt tired and dizzy, and I was waking up with headaches. I did not think much of the symptoms, because I had passed having a healthy pregnancy up to this point. I thought what I was feeling was normal, especially being that I was in my mid-thirties. I remember my friend Agnes telling me to get checked. She said didn't think I looked well. I decided to wait for my appointment, which was Friday of that week, not thinking that what I was feeling was real sickness. Come the morning of the appointment with my gynecologist, I was five weeks away from having Baby Sally. I had skipped my previous appointment because Nate was sick. I hadn't rescheduled because, as a single mom, I was focused on working as much as I could to save for maternity leave when the baby was born. Since my doctor was always happy with my health, I stupidly chose to work when I had a doctor's appointment.

On this morning, I had scheduled an early morning appointment to enable me to get to work in time for my work-related appointments that day. I was confused about locations since I had scheduled my doctor's appointment based on the location that coincided with my work appointments. When I went to see my doctor, I found myself at the wrong location. The people there redirected me to the right location. I drove there as fast as I could, because I had a work-related home-care appointment at 11:00 a.m. I was getting anxious because I did not want to be late for work. When I got to the right location, I was too late for my doctor's appointment. There were five women waiting to be seen. I was told that my doctor could see me after seeing the five other women. Looking at time, which was about nine thirty, I asked the receptionist to reschedule my appointment for the following week. I needed to be at work by eleven. She looked at my record and stated that she would recommend I be seen on that day, seeing as I had missed my previous appointment. I insisted that I had to go to work. I said that I could come back in as soon as she could schedule me, on a different day.

All of a sudden, one of the pregnant women waiting came forward and said, "I have time and I can wait." She said she was next in line. I could be seen in her place, and she would wait for my turn. I was in a hurry because I had scheduled a visit on this day. That was totally God's saving voice speaking through her. I was resisting because time was still moving, but the woman at the desk said she was going to check to find out if I could be seen right away. I placed a call to the patient as I was a hospice chaplain house and let him know I was going to be late. The receptionist came back and said I could be seen, so I was taken to the back right away. As soon as the nurse took my blood pressure, her eyes opened wide. I had no idea what she was thinking. I just wanted to get out of there. She said that the doctor needed to see me right away, and then she walked out. In no time, she came back with the doctor.

The doctor checked me out and stated that I needed an ultrasound right away. I was going nuts because I was going to be late for work. I let the doctor know that I needed to be at work. She stated, "You are not going to work!"

What?! I thought. The doctor and the nurse were busy checking me out while many thoughts went through my mind in the space of a few seconds. I asked what was going on, as everyone in the room looked puzzled. I did not think I was sick. They told me I had preeclampsia and the baby had to delivered as soon as possible. I had never heard of preeclampsia and had no idea what that meant. I told the doctor that I was worried about my son. I told her I needed to make appropriate arrangements for him before I could be hospitalized. She said I did not have time and could not leave. She said I needed to get to the hospital right away and that I would be given more instructions at the hospital. The staff asked me who had brought me to the doctor's office, and of course I had come alone. In my mind, they were making a big deal out of it. I said I could take myself to the hospital, which was just across the street. I did end up doing that. I was hopeful that the hospital staff would let me go home and do what I needed to get done. On my way to the hospital, I called the hospice patient's home, apologized for the wait, and let him know I wasn't going to make it for the visit that day. I called work and let them know I was not going to be coming to work that day. I called to check on my son; he was okay. I still did not have an understanding of what was happening. I was not convinced I was going to have my baby that day.

When I got to the prenatal care section of the hospital, medical practitioners were waiting for me. They did another ultrasound and said I needed to get to an operating room immediately. I panicked. I had so many questions. By this time, everybody was rushing and no one was really talking to me. I was yelled at to sign the permission slip, because I was resisting doing so. I did not have a clear understanding of what all of this meant. I remember the doctor saying that my baby's heart rate was dropping steadily and that my blood pressure was dangerously high. She said we were both in danger of dying, so they were going to do an emergency C-section to try to save us. I could not believe what I was hearing. By that time they had an IV in me with magnesium, I requested to call someone concerning my son, which the hospital staff let me do as they continued to prepare me. I called my friend Agnes and asked her to pick up Nate, and to keep him until further notice. I let her know I was in the hospital and that things were not looking good. I told her that I could not talk much. I then called my spiritual mom, Joan, and she set on her way to the hospital. No more of my questions were answered after that. All I remember was people running next to me as I was on a gurney. I had started feeling drowsy, which I believe was from the magnesium. As soon as I was done with those two quick calls, an anesthetist put a mask over my face. I fought it. I had planned to have local anesthesia for my C-section, like I did with Nate, not general anesthesia. That was what I was trying to let the hospital staff know, but I was out before I knew it. I found out later that they don't do local anesthesia for emergency surgeries.

The first thing I remember being told once I awoke was that I had a very tiny baby girl. I was in and out as the staff wheeled me through the NICU, where my daughter was. I remember touching her little fingers through the vent and calling her name, Sally. That was all I remember. I was wheeled to my room. The doctor came to talk to me and informed me that they were planning on putting a feeding tube in my daughter, who weighed only two pounds. He said they were also going to put in an oxygen tube to help her breathe. He said they were, however, not worried about her anymore, but they were concerned about me. He said I needed to relax and rest because my blood pressure was still dangerously high. I was drugged and had trouble comprehending everything I was being told, but I felt terrible about hearing that they were worried about my life. Thankfully, Joan was with me that evening, which was very helpful.

After Joan left that evening, I was left in my solitude. The desperation that filled my spirit was greater than any I'd ever imagined. I could not cry if I wanted to. I did not have energy to do anything, yet all I wanted was to see my two children. I could not go to either of them, and neither of them could come to me at that moment. As worry started to fill my heart, I remembered to pray. I could not imagine my two children being in the situations they were in without having their mother present. I was afraid to sleep. I remember I had my hospital bed cranked up to a sitting position. I prayed compulsively until my mind couldn't stay awake any longer. I have no idea when I finally fell asleep. The next morning found me in a better place overall, and the medical staff were not as worried for my life as they had been the previous night. However, the magnesium had started messing with my cognition. I did not like how it made me feel. On that morning, I was able to get clear explanations about what had taken place on the previous day. It was all shocking to hear. I was informed that I was likely to have been found dead had my baby not been delivered the previous day. The doctors highly doubted I would have made it through the night if I hadn't gotten immediate help. I had preeclampsia with HELLP syndrome. My blood pressure was 196 over 98, which they said put me at risk for a stroke, among other things. It was shocking to hear all this and to realize that my daughter and I were dying when we got rescued. Sally's heart rate had dropped to a dangerous level by the time she was delivered. The preeclampsia had also caused her to not receive nutrition for a period before delivery which had caused her to loss weight while in the womb. At the time I was hearing all these things, I had not seen her that morning. All I wanted to do was to see her.

The best of what happened that day was when I held my daughter in my arms for the first time. She was so little, there was almost nothing to hold. A two-pound baby, she was perfect. I was very happy. The surprise was that Sally did not have any tubes in her, as I was expecting, based on what I had been told the previous night. A nurse informed me that Sally did not need any interventions other than the incubator to keep her warm. She started to look for food right away and ate safely when she fed. She did not need oxygen, as she was breathing on her own. That was my miracle and God's grace on me, because I was going through a really tough time with my son. God saved me from having to deal with two children who had complications. On that day, my friend Agnes brought Nate to see his sister. I was blessed to spend some time with both of my children, which felt like a dream compared to my previous night's struggle and worries. Agnes was gracious to bring Nate to the hospital every day I remained in the hospital, which meant more to me than my heart can express.

Thinking of all that had happened in my life within the space of a single day was very overwhelming. I wished I could meet with the woman who had given me her appointment time to be seen. I wished she knew that she saved the lives of two people by her act of kindness. My heart was also filled with gratitude for the doctor who saved both my life and Sally's life. I will never forget how that doctor looks or how determined she was to save us even though I was in such a fog. Everyone was so kind, which was completely God's intervention. My heart was forever humbled to realize that I had been in such a vulnerable position and that it took many wonderful people to save my life while I had lost control over everything. I felt blessed for having been taken care of for a period of about twenty-four hours by a group of people I did not get to know at all. I thank God for speaking to the woman who gave up her turn at the clinic for my sake, and for all the people involved in saving me and Sally. As a result of my yielding while my whole being was convincing me to go to work, my daughter and I survived and thrived.

Hanging on for My Life

Many times in my life as a hospice chaplain, I encountered patients who would not lie down to sleep. This happened especially when death drew closer. These people often would say they were afraid to lie down because they were afraid of not awaking again. They were afraid to die. They wanted to stay in a sitting position. Even when they would snooze and almost fall out of bed, I could not convince them that lying down actually helps. The only way I got to understand them was by going through a similar experience.

When the doctor gives you a report that you are facing death, especially when you least expect it or least want to hear it, it turns your entire world upside down. It is in this moment of your life that you come to terms with what really matters. I had just experienced an emergency C-section along with preeclampsia, the latter of which the doctors said could have killed me. While I was in the hospital, I felt that the harder I prayed, the more God was bound to hear my prayers. I had my hospital bed cranked to an upright position, as I had seen many of our patients at Hospice of the Twin Cities do, which action never made sense to me. This time, it made perfect sense to me, as I was fighting for my own life. There was no way that the bed was going down that night. I was afraid. It felt like I was dying when I thought of putting the bed down to a flat position. All I was thinking about was my children. I pleaded and pleaded as if God needed me to plead with Him. But that was what I needed to do; nothing else mattered except pleading with God to help me raise my children. I had my eyes wide open. The more I struggled to keep myself awake, the wider I wanted to open my eyes. I did not want to fall asleep. I felt like I needed to stay awake to make sure I didn't die. That night, I didn't remember what it meant to surrender to God. What made sense to me was to fight for my life by not allowing myself to fall asleep. I did not know at what time I eventually fell asleep, but I am glad I did. I awoke the next morning feeling better.

That was the most humbling of all the experiences of my life. I did not realize how precious life was until that day. I came to terms with the fact that life is a gift and that, no matter how good you feel, things can change within the twinkling of an eye. After going through that experience, I made new decisions concerning my life. I decided to live every day as if it were the last day I had here on earth. My children were precious to me, but I had a new understanding of what time with them meant. I came to a new understanding of how much I loved them and didn't what them to grow without the love of their mother. I thought more about the calling on my heart for orphans and abandoned children. The many children growing up without anyone to care for them became more real to my heart. I started focusing more on my calling than I had done in previous years. Meanwhile, at the hospice where I worked, I had a new understanding of what people went through when they were not wanting to lie down or close their eyes during their dying days. It moved me from a place of not understanding to a place of empathy when I encountered the same thing myself.

The God of Impossibilities

"And looking at them Jesus said to them, 'With people this is impossible, but with God all things are possible'" (Matthew 19:26 NASB).

Growing up as a young woman, I had a desire to be married and have children. Yes, I got married, and my marriage ended up in separation followed by divorce. Coming from a culture that did not much mention divorce, I thought I was finished for a while. I lost my status with many people, including those close and dear to me. Then followed an out-of-wedlock baby. That nailed it. I became an outcast to many. I was a divorced single mother of two children. Culturally, I was completely doomed as far as ever dreaming of having a husband goes. To make matters worse, one of my children had medical struggles that made the hospital our second home and my other child was a two-pound premature baby. Many people could not bear me anymore because I was too much to handle. I am thankful that while people judge by the external, God judges the heart. His grace was sufficient. He was with me through it all, and I saw Him move on a daily basis.

The time of my pregnancy with my daughter, I was more alone than at any other time of my life. It was a season of solitude; I engaged with people minimally. During this period of time, I prayed a lot and reevaluated my life. Why had my life turned out to be so sour? Why did everything seem to go wrong? Why was there so much pain in my life, and how much more could I bear? I cried a lot during the first month of the pregnancy, but God picked me up and started mending my heart again. I asked God to forgive me for my sins and for the image I had created of myself as a minister of the gospel. God started to heal my heart and helped me to forgive myself. I needed to forgive myself, because I had a child in me who did not deserve my emotional distress. I am glad I humbled my heart and accepted God's grace and mercy again. As I opened my heart to God, He started to show me things about myself that I had never paid attention to before. I did not value myself as much as I believed I did. I had never really let myself think about what I really wanted in life. I did not believe I deserved to be cared for by anybody. Since I am naturally a caregiver, I thought it was always my role to provide the care in every relationship. I was afraid to have a stable man in my life, so I went the opposite direction time and again. The surprise to me was instead of being appreciated, I was abused and taken advantage of. I started to see some of the choices I had made and the people I had been around. I was abused physically, verbally, and emotionally, and I blame it all on the fact that I got life wrong. My self-deception about what being a good woman was led me down this ugly path of life.

As I continued to search God for healing in solitude, I started to embrace myself as important and worthy of a good life. In the past, I had felt like I had to pay my way through life wherever I was. God showed me that He had paid my way many years ago. He showed me that I am His daughter, deserving of all He has in store for His children. I had these revelations during my pregnancy with Sally. I made new decisions concerning my life during this pregnancy. I completely stopped caring whether I ever was going to get married again. Marriage was the message preached to me all my life. It's not an easy idea to get rid of. All of a sudden, God delivered me, so being married no longer mattered to my heart. I stopped worrying what people thought of me, said to me, and said about me. It no longer mattered that many looked down on me. While many were busy judging me, God was busy restoring me. He helped me deal with my shame. I started making plans for how I was going to move forward. I had a good job and some support from people, some of whom I did not expect it from. My place of work and my coworkers at the time were very supportive when I needed their support most.

After having my baby, I started to pray again. I asked God what I should do. I remember this question falling on my heart: "What do you really want?" I was confused for a moment. I remember thinking, *Me, Lord? What do I want?* That was an interesting question, so I sat on it. I did not think that I had a choice at that moment. As I processed the question in my heart, the story of the paralyzed man at the pool of Bethesda came to my heart, John 5:1–18. The man had been paralyzed for thirty-eight years. Jesus asked him a question, "Do you want to get well?", and the man's condition in no time became history for him. Faith filled my heart all of a sudden. What did I really want? My desire for marriage surfaced again. My desire for my children to have a dad surfaced. I was on my maternity leave. As insane as it sounded then, I gave God my answer: I wanted a husband and a dad for my children. The next question that came to my heart was one of what I wanted in that package. I went to my knees and prayed as I thought in my heart. I took a piece of paper and wrote ten of the most important things I would like to have in a husband. I prayed over those things. I dared God.

In a month after praying that prayer, I met my husband Steve. I totally believe this had to do with the blessing my father had given me while I was pregnant with my daughter, a few months before this moment. In the midst of my most miserable condition, God showed up. My son was still struggling medically, and my daughter was a tiny three-month-old preemie. God blew my mind. He did not just bring into my life any man. He brought into my life a man who fit the description of what I had asked in my prayer. It made me start doubting what was happening. Thankfully, God had worked so much in me that I was a different person than I had ever known myself to be. When doubt started to build and I started to think that my relationship with Steve was too good to be true, I was reminded of Acts 12:5–17. In that Scripture, the believers were praying for the impossible in their mind. They asked God to release Peter from prison. When Peter stood at the door after God released him from prison, the believers who had been crying to God ran away, calling Peter a ghost. This encouraged my heart to keep moving forward. In the past, I worked for relationships and paid for them. This time, I had made up my mind that I was okay with never being with a man. I had decided that I was only going to be with a man who valued me and saw me from God's point of view.

In spite of my circumstances, I didn't pursue Steve. He pursued me from day one. The only times when I went to find him was when I wanted to make sure he was where he said he would be. Other than that, he was the one who came to me—and he was consistent. Our dates were over the lunch hour, and he paid for each and every date. I totally let him be the man as I watched his moves closely. I had met people who admired me but then left me the moment they discovered how difficult my life was with my son's medical problems. Right away I told Steve about my journey with my son, because I wanted him to leave me then if he was going to at all. He did not leave. He believed he had found in me what he was looking for in a woman. He wanted to know me more.

I remember talking to Steve from the hospital in our early days after meeting. My son was undergoing a brain surgery, and my daughter, who was about three months old, lay beside me on a guest couch in my son's hospital room. I did not invite Steve to come to the hospital, because I had not gotten to know him well yet. He called me regularly to check on us; I never called him during that time. I had no idea how our relationship was going to turn out, but I had opened up to try it, because Steve seemed right in the way he handled things with me. Little did I know that he was going to marry me in eight months from the time of our first meeting. What I respect most about Steve is that he loved me for the real me. I did not share much of my positive life or my future dreams with him at that time. He probably would not have believed me then anyway, given how complicated my circumstances were. I knew I was going to be okay eventually. I believed that if my circumstances did not kill me, they would make me stronger, but Steve didn't know that. He fell in love with the person I was. And in spite of everything he could see about my life, he treated me like a princess from the beginning. He respected my boundaries and treated me with love and affection. While all that meant the world to me, what I really fell in love with was how intimate he is. We related with each other deeply. When we started seeing each other outside of our lunch hours, we spent a lot of time talking, mostly about spiritual things. Very deeply, we just knew we were meant to be. We never went to watch a movie or sat and watched TV during our courtship. We loved and enjoyed every moment of talking to each other, and we seemed to find quiet places in the park to spend time talking.

My husband has been a real man to me, and I have a great deal of respect for him. When the minister who joined us in marriage asked Steve why he chose to marry me, Steve said it was because I challenged him. That answer surprised me, because I had no idea that was the case. I was just being myself. I had come to know who I was in God's sight, and I was not settling anymore. I believe that if I had not reached a place of being whole as a person, I would have missed out on Steve, because he was very specific in what he prayed for in a wife. I share all of this because I want other women in tough situations to know that our circumstances cannot limit God. If He did this for me, He can do it for you. God knows no impossibility.

Years later, Steve's and my love for each other continues to grow deeper and wider. He is a good-hearted man who loves God. He is not a perfect man, just like I am not a perfect woman. He has a past and a story just like I do. Our circumstances together have not been perfect, but we have a great relationship. Together we continue to grow in ways of the Lord. We both look to change and develop our lives, and we support each other in our daily journey. Nate and Sally completely love Steve, respect him, and look up to him. Steve loves children naturally, so he gives Nate and Sally consistent attention. We read the Bible together every day and pray together as a family before the kids go to bed for the night. We go to church every Sunday because it is important to my husband and me, which means the children get to attend church every Sunday. My prayer is that as Nate and Sally continue to grow while watching my and Steve's commitment to God, they will develop their own commitment to and walk with God. Under extreme circumstances, I was married, a second time, to a good husband, and now my children have the love of a dependable dad. Only God could have made this possible.

Divine Comfort

What are the chances that a neurosurgeon from the Mayo Clinic in Rochester, Minnesota, plans a trip to volunteer in a specific country in Africa and that his future patient from the United States, without any knowledge of the neurosurgeon's trip, plans a trip to the same country at the very same time?

After our family had canceled one trip to Kenya the previous year, we didn't want to cancel the next one if we didn't have to. My son, Nate, had gotten sick three weeks before our planned trip to Kenya. We ended up in an ER close to home, after which time we had to take him to the Mayo Clinic to see his surgeon, Dr. Wetjen. Nate had gone through a major brain surgery the previous year. With Nate's now being sick, our family started wondering whether it was safe to travel to Kenya. Dr. Wetjen checked Nate out and then said that he felt comfortable with Nate's status. He also broke to us some news that we did not expect to hear at all: he was traveling to Kenya and would be there for two of the four weeks we were going. What a miracle! He told us not worry, saying that if anything happened to Nate while we were in Kenya, he (Dr. Wetjen) would be there for him. Dr. Wetjen then let us know how to contact him. It was such an act of kindness. We traveled to Kenya filled with peace and comfort.

The trip was fabulous. Nate did very well for the entire time of our trip. But what meant the most to us all was the peace of mind in knowing that we were not alone in Kenya at that time. God has a way of organizing things on our behalf before we know we need those things. We had contemplated canceling our trip for the second time. If Nate's surgeon had said it was the right thing to do, then we would have canceled it. Not only did Dr. Wetjen reassure us concerning Nate's status, making us feel okay about traveling, but also God worked out the details of that trip and multiplied our peace. Being that I know my way in Kenya, we had God's favor to see our son's neurosurgeon on the other side of the world. We did not take that lightly. We thank God for it, and we thank Dr. Wetjen for giving us that honor. God revealed to us through this experience that we should always praise Him, even when things seem dark. We already had bought our tickets and were scheduled to travel in three weeks. We first felt devastated when Nate got sick, especially when remembering that we had changed our travel plans the previous year. But shortly God gave us peace. We especially encouraged Nate not to feel like it was his fault if we needed to cancel the trip. Little did we know that what the Enemy had planned to use against us, God took it and turned it around to bless us. If Nate had not gotten sick at that time, then we may not have been blessed with the amazing experience of that trip. God cares about the details of our lives more than we can imagine.

Part Two.

A word to hold onto.

Expression of Faithfulness

Look at the sun
As she makes her way
Through the beautiful skies.
Her rays smiling gloriously
Are seen by all alike.
Her warmth, like a blanket,
Is felt equally by all.

Look at the sun
Rising in the morning,
Always from the east,
Never from the north.
She strolls across the sky
Gently like a dove,
Seen by all alike.

Look at the sun
Setting in the evening,
The colors that surround her
As beautiful as can be.
She vanishes shyly
As though aware
Of millions of eyes watching.

Look at the sun,
Never changing her course,
Trustworthy to lead the way,
Dependable to brighten all,
Consistent in everything.
In her life we find the
True expression of faithfulness.

—Ann Makena

The Background Story

I was five months pregnant with Nathanael when the doctor ordered a routine ultrasound. I did not have any complications, so I hadn't expected any of what was going to come my way that day. I had been praying to God and speaking to Nathanael by his name since the day I had found out I was pregnant with him, which was when I was about six weeks pregnant. When I had told people I was expecting Nathanael before I had the ultrasound, they laughed as one would expect. Some even teased me about having a girl called Nathanael, but I had no doubt in my mind that the child I was carrying was male. The ultrasound confirmed this, revealing it was a boy. However, with that good news came some bad news. The ultrasound technician told me that something was wrong with the baby.

I met with my doctor shortly after that, and he sadly told me he did not expect the child to make it to full term. He informed me that the child's brain was worse than any he had ever seen in the years of his medical practice. He talked about the details of what he saw, which included multiple brain malformations: the brain's outer lobes (cortex) and the drainage system (ventricles) were not formed correctly. There were other complications as well. The doctor told me that he saw no need for me to go through the pain of trying to carry this pregnancy to term, because he expected the baby to die in my womb any day, based on his experience. He told me he had seen similar cases and that those children ended up not growing like other children, but those children's situations were not even close to how bad my unborn child's situation was. That was the beginning of the testing of the faith I had in God when it came to Nathanael, given the things I had seen in my spirit. The amazing thing was that I did not feel afraid concerning Nate. Instead, I was in shock, unable to process what I was seeing with my eyes and what I was hearing with my ears. There was peace in my heart, a peace that I couldn't reconcile with what the doctor was telling me. When I focused on my heart, I saw Nathanael living, walking, talking, playing, etc.

I felt right away that what I was experiencing was warfare; therefore, I let my doctor know that I was going to have my baby. My doctor and the ultrasound technician showed me the images of Nate's brain again and persuaded me to believe them. I believed them because I could see it with my own eyes, although I did not understand all of the medical implications. I wished the doctor could see where I was coming from. I did not want him to feel that I doubted his professional experience. Yet at that moment, there were two things I saw. One of these things I saw in my spirit, and the other I saw with my natural eyes. I had no doubt that Nathanael was going to live. I did not know how he would, but I felt such a confidence in my spirit that such would be the case. The doctor was frustrated with me and asked me why I wanted to continue a pregnancy that would end with the baby dead in my womb. He continued, telling me that if any miracle brought this baby to term, the baby would not live past the first hour after birth. Logically, it was very shocking for me to hear all these things. I expected all good news, since I believed that God had a purpose for Nathanael. What the doctor said made sense to my psyche, but it didn't make sense to my heart. Other specialists had talked to me about their experience with hope in order to convince me of how bad things were. I could understand where they were coming from, seeing as they are experienced in what they do. But I had no way of helping them to understand where I was coming from. In my spirit, I did not see an end to Nathanael. He was a gift from God. He was supposed to be naturally and uniquely godly from the time of his birth.

I do have a respect for doctors. Even in this case, I did not think different of them. I wished they could see what I was seeing though, just as they had showed me what they were talking about. The one thing that remained in my heart that I believed deeply and couldn't prove to anyone was that Nathanael had a destiny. I told my doctor that I wanted to leave the outcome my pregnancy to God. The doctor stated in frustration, which I totally understood (because he cared), "Let's see what God will do!" I remember his words as if they had been spoken just yesterday. At the moment of the doctor's declaration, I surrendered my pregnancy to God.

Since my mind was made up, I decided to have a fresh start. I chose to work with a different doctor, one who had not been involved with me yet. I informed the new doctor that I was aware of what my previous health care providers thought. I understood why the other doctor said what he did, and I had no ill feelings toward him. I just did not want to continue hearing that my child was dying. In fact, I didn't want to hear anything else that my previous doctor said. I wanted to completely keep the results of my pregnancy out of my hands. I had to trust One who was greater than I, namely God. I requested Him to help me deliver my baby in the safest way.

My new doctor suggested a C-section to avoid brain trauma during the birth. Moving forward, I saw the doctor weekly until Nathanael was born, to make sure he was alive each week. I had orders to have an ultrasound monthly as well. I did not have any other complications with the pregnancy. Nathanael was delivered safely as scheduled, one week before his due date. I was able to work until the last week before having him, and I never missed a day of work during that time, except for the ones I had scheduled to take off. God gave me amazing grace and joy throughout the pregnancy. I did not share the doctor's report with my coworkers or with most other people, including my family. I believe that the more you talk about something, the more warfare you face. People may not have bad intentions in what they say many times, but the fact remains that there is power in words, no matter what the intention is. All I wanted was God's word to be declared and for positive things to be said about Nathanael. Therefore, I shared the doctor's report with only a handful of people, including my pastor, some members of my family, and some of my friends. These were people I trusted not to spread what the doctors had said, not to worry about my pregnancy, and not to talk about the death of my unborn baby as a possibility. I expected them to stand with me in prayer, believing God for His word concerning Nathanael.

The Word

Life is not easy, and it should not be expected to be easy. No matter what our life situation is, we will be faced with difficult choices throughout our life journey. Having a word from God for each situation helps in making the choice that leaves a person peaceful, even when it is not an easy choice.

I cannot boast that I was strong in deciding to have Nathanael after I was assured and reassured by medical professionals that he was not going to reach term. I did not any think that the doctors didn't know what they were talking about. Professionally they were right, because they deal with this type of situation on a regular basis. However, I had a word from the greatest One of all concerning Nathanael. Before I was pregnant with Nathanael, I was reading John 1:43–50, which is about Nathanael, when it was laid on my heart that Nathanael would be my son's name. Once I found out I was pregnant, the same impression came to my heart, reminding me of that name. Although I received no details along with the word, what I saw from the ultrasound did not dislodge what was in my heart. The words were clear, peaceful, and joyful. Immediately I knew I was carrying Nathanael in my body. I started praying for him by using his name, as was placed in my heart. Little did I know that the Enemy was going to attack my unborn child's life. I believe it wasn't in God's will for Nathanael to have brain problems, but God did allow it to happen.

The word that God had spoken to me was what made me confident to go ahead and have Nathanael. There have been many times during the journey of raising Nate that life got rough and I felt like I was ready to crumple into a heap. I had moments when I felt very alone. Other times I got very tired physically, emotionally, and mentally. Even spiritually, I got so tired that I could not pray. But the word placed in my heart concerning my child kept me going. Over time, it made sense to me that God never promises us that life will be easy. What He promises is to be with us. I can truly testify that I have seen God at work through this process. Also, it was revealed to me why God doesn't tell us what we will go through when He gives us His word. If I had known at the beginning what the journey was going to be like, I would have probably fallen flat and died instantly. However, although the road has been rough, God's grace has been sufficient. I have never regretted having Nathanael. This child is such a precious gift that I am confident I would do it again for him by God's grace. These are the mysteries of faith. I have grown and have learned so much from raising my son. Doing so has made me a much better person, one who is more useful for God's kingdom. One thing I can truly say is that God is faithful and that He watches over His Word to perform it.

Having a word for Nathanael also helped me not take people's negative words and behavior personally. It has also helped me to do my part and to surrender the rest to God. My part is to raise Nathanael in God's ways. The outcome of Nathanael's life is all in

God's hands. This is a peaceful truth, one that has kept me very calm in situations where I would have otherwise worn my pants on my head. I have had to fight some battles, and I have had to stand up as an advocate for my child when I felt it was my parental responsibility. Nate's life has been one of tough warfare, and I have found myself on my knees a lot. I have depended on God in order to show those people involved in our lives what our needs are. If I did so myself, then those around me would be tired of listening to me. And God has been faithful. This has kept me from having to fight too hard physically for my child. I surrendered Nathanael to God before he was born. Many times when I have been tempted to take my son's life into my own hands, I only have to look back at what God has done. Nate is my child to enjoy while I raise him. He is also God's child, whose task is to fulfill the purpose for which God has him here on earth.

I have also learned that God speaks differently in every situation and in different people's lives. He has taught me to pray and to be careful to discern what He is wanting to happen in each situation I face. God has taught me not to build any expectation based on another situation or someone else's experience of Him. God is very creative and does not run out of new ideas. The surest way to discern God's word for your life is by making sure it matches His Word, the Bible. What God speaks to our heart will contradict His written Word. This motivates me to read the Bible and to meditate on it in order to understand what it means. I also read the Bible to receive encouragement.

Mary was told that she was going to give birth to the Savior of the World. My imagination tells me that Mary did not expect to see her child go through what she watched Him go through during His entire life here on earth. Her focus on what God had spoken to her kept her going. She left the outcome of her child's life to God.

Moses was called a deliverer, yet he was abandoned in a river and also spent forty years in the wilderness. Delivering the children of Israel was not easy for Moses. David was imperfect, yet God called him a man after His own heart. The lives of these people, among others, are powerful teachings of how mysterious God is.

Experiencing God at work in my life prior to having Nate helped me have the confidence to trust Him again. Having friends like Joan and Mary (who I met at church when I was new In the U.S. and she became great support to me), and having my family, was very helpful, because all of them knew what was going on. Together we confessed God's Word over Nathanael's life throughout my pregnancy. In many of the Bible stories, God silenced those who doubted or who spoke words of doubt. He commanded Joshua not to let anyone who spoke doubt speak at all. He silenced Zachariah for his expressing doubt that his wife at an old age was going to have a child. Avoiding spread of doubt instead of faith, is the reason I choose not to share my struggles publicly but only with those that will hold onto faith with me.

God is faithful to His Word in His own way. Instead of spending energy trying to understand God, I learned to stretch out my hand, reach out for His hand, and let Him lead me step by step. God has shown me things about Nathanael that I could not fathom, given what was happening in the natural world. He fulfilled His word by causing the unaffected parts of Nathanael's brain to overcompensate so that he functions like other children his age. Our God is the unlimited God.

On the Tough Days

The only days I experienced sadness during my pregnancy with Nathanael were the day when I had an ultrasound. God works mysteriously. The head of the gynecology department at the hospital where I received treatment did my ultrasounds every month. He was a Christian believer. Although he couldn't keep the ultrasound images from me, he was sensitive and supportive, which was very helpful. On those days, I was reminded of what Nate's brain looked like. That was very difficult to see, humanly speaking. It was also very disappointing and depressing, because I kept trusting that God would perform a miracle since He had spoken to my heart concerning Nathanael. I always prayed before the next ultrasound that my son's brain would be made normal, but that did not happen. The next time, it would be the same as it was last time. On those days, I went home and cried out to God, not knowing what to pray. The only thing that happened each time was that God's peace filled my heart. I kept reading the Word of God to seek strength.

As humans, we want God to answer our prayers according to our limited perception. We forget that God is unlimited. Isaiah 55:8–9 states, "'For My thoughts are not your thoughts, Nor are your ways My ways,' declares the Lord. 'For as the heavens are higher than the earth, So are My ways higher than your ways And My thoughts than your thoughts.'" The day after one of my ultrasounds, I found myself continuing with life and going to work with joy as usual. What has come to pass is that the functioning parts of Nathanael's brain have overcompensated in ways that were unexpected. God did not change things physically for my son, but He made what Nate had available work miraculously.

Faith Must Have Action: The Crib

Putting up the crib as an act of faith

I was in the fifth month of my pregnancy when the doctors stopped talking to me about their grim expectations for my son. We were now on the same page; they were going to help me have Nathanael. I was reminded that faith without works is dead (James 2:14–26).

> What good is it, my brothers, if someone says he has faith but does not have works? Can that faith save him? If a brother or sister is poorly clothed and lacking in daily food, and one of you says to them, "Go in peace, be warmed and filled," without giving them the things needed for the body, what good is that? So also faith by itself, if it does not have works, is dead.

I felt strongly in my heart that I wanted a crib in my home for Nathanael. Once I had brought a crib home, I wanted it out of the box and ready. I put bedding in the crib and bought some clothes for my son, putting them in his bedroom-to-be. Although this might not make sense to some people, it made perfect sense to my heart. I stood in that bedroom every day, several times a day, dreaming, praying, and thanking God for Nathanael. As I stood there, I saw Nathaniel in the crib, sleeping, standing, and calling out. I also saw him as older, walking out of his bedroom. I did this every day of the remaining months of my pregnancy, until the day he was born. While I was still pregnant, different people held three different baby showers for Nate. All of them were surprise. If only these people had known what was expected for Nathanael! By the time he was born, he had everything he needed or wanted. My apartment was packed with baby stuff. (The clothes and diapers and gift cards lasted us a full year after Nate was born, and some things lasted much longer, which was God's unexpected provision.) Mary and Joan who were holding faith with me planned one of the three showers. The other showers were planned by people who had no idea the baby was not expected to survive and were surprise showers. I felt that this was God's way of confirming to me, through His people, that He was involved.

The Long-Awaited Day Arrives

At the time of Nate's birth, my doctors reminded me of what they had already informed me of earlier: that is if my baby made it to term, he was not expected to cry after birth and was not expected to survive past the first hour of his life. I had a local C-section and was alert when Nathanael was delivered. I felt that the team who delivered Nate were professional and did their very best to maintain safety in spite of what they thought was going to happen. Nate was comfortable in my womb and not yet ready to be born. It was a bit of struggle to pull him down, since he was very high in my womb. Once my surgeon had him out and in his hands, Nathanael, to that doctor's surprise, let out a huge scream right away. He was extremely loud. I remember that a staff member exclaimed, "He's got some strong lungs!" Absolutely no intervention was needed for Nathanael's delivery, apart from the C-section.

I remember the way the doctor held up Nate in surprise. Nathanael screamed to the team's amazement. He was not expected to cry, let alone do it without any sort of intervention. He was taken to the ICU after I had had a chance to touch him and give him a kiss, as I was still on the operating table. He lived past the first hour of birth and then started showing signs that he wanted to eat. The staff fed him. He ate like any other baby and did not have any complication. He breathed by himself without any complications. Again, he did not need any intervention in the ICU other than monitoring.

On the same day that Nate was born, my pastor, Randy, and my friends Mary and Joan, who had all known exactly what was going on, were there to support us, I will forever be thankful for that. Other friends who were close to us came too, which made it a happy celebration of the arrival of Nathanael. The next day, after Nate's birth, I was able to hold him in my arms and breastfeed him with no complications.

I do not recall at what point the doctors decided that Nathanael needed to be transferred to a children's hospital that specialized in placing shunts in the brain. He was aligned with one of the best-known brain surgeons in the country in dealing with hydrocephalus, Dr. Nagib. After his birth on a Thursday morning,

Nate lived without intervention for his first four days. He was then transferred to Children's Hospitals and Clinics of Minnesota on the following Sunday. Nathanael had his first brain surgery when he was five days old, on the same day I was discharged from the hospital after the C-section. Although I felt every bump as I was wheeled in a wheelchair that day, I was very thankful to be with my child right after his first surgery. After making a quick recovery from the surgery, Nathanael continued to grow as any other child. He was discharged from the hospital two weeks later, with no further complications or interventions. In the natural, that was surprising!

Home Was Ready for My Baby

At two weeks, Nathanael was discharged to go home, and home was ready for him. Included in the package was my sister Lucy, who had sacrificed so much and had come all the way from Kenya to help me out during such a time of need. (Sister Lucy stayed with us for four months, at which time I was strong enough to continue on my own.) I was excited to bring Nate home at last. I had managed to go to the hospital every day when he was an inpatient, which helped prepare me to bring him home. Many people came to see Nathanael once he was home, showering him with gifts upon gifts. Nathanael knew no lack, thanks to God's provisions through my friends. He continued to grow normally as our family and friends continued to hold him in faith. The doctors were not expecting much of Nate based on his brain damage. To everyone's amazement, however, Nathanael was not late for, and did not miss, a single milestone as a baby.

Nathanael's pediatrician pronounced him a normal child at the age of two years. She stated to me, "Nathanael is a normal child and should be treated as a normal child." Nathanael miraculously had proved himself enough that there was no more doubt. By this time, he had gone through two shunt revisions, but these did not affect his growth. He did not have any other medical concerns and was not on any medications until he reached the age of six and half years, which is when he started the battle with seizures. That was not easy to endure.

Even though our had faith in God, we experienced many times of worry. Through it all, God remained present and faithful. I was separated legally from my first husband when Nathanael was two and half years old. After that, I was divorced. From the time Nathanael was two and a half years old, I raised him as a single mother by myself or with the help of my family. Life has been challenging in many ways, but God has been with us. As I mentioned before, He never promised us that life would be easy, but He did promise to be with us.

God Works Mysteriously

Here I was, a single mother with a son who had a tough medical condition, not much family around other than the times a family member came to help from time to time, (since my family were all in Kenya), and a lot of hospital visits and admissions. I was a full-time student, struggling to keep my job. What I didn't keep in mind at that time was that God had everything all figured out for me. When Nathanael was about two years old, he was scheduled for another brain surgery, this one to revise the shunt again. At the same time, I was on my way to being separated from my first husband. On top of being a full-time student, I worked three overnight shifts a week to enable me to be home with Nathanael during the day. It was a testing time because I had made up my mind to separate from my first husband when I was informed that Nathanael needed surgery. I could have made the choice not to separate based on my needs, but I felt that I had to move on the separation for the reasons I had decided on earlier. I had a big problem facing me. At first I wondered how I was going to make it after the separation took place, but I moved forward with the plan in spite of my uncertainty about the future. It is during our moments of stepping out of what we believe to be our comfort zone in faith when God moves on our behalf. He was on time when I took a step of faith and trusted Him.

I am very thankful for my family, who have been very supportive of me throughout my life. My mom and dad decided that mom be the one to travel from Kenya to help me out this time, since my sister Lucy had come when Nathanael was first born. My mom ended up staying with me for a full year and a half. I don't know what I would have done without her. I thank God for my dad, too, who was very supportive of me during this time and who encouraged my mother to stay in the United States until things settled down with me. That was such a huge sacrifice on my dad's part, one that was made in love.

My mother was with me when I separated from my first husband and during Nate's surgery. Nate ended up having two other brain surgeries, for a total of three, during the time my mother was with me. This was one of the ways God came through for us. From the time of Nathanael's birth until he was two and half years old, he had undergone a total of seven brain surgeries. God unexpectedly provided me with a job that worked perfectly for my circumstances within this time frame. I did not look for that job. By way of a miracle, the job found me—and paid me much more than what I was earning before. This job also worked perfectly with Nate's school schedule, when that time came. Nathanael was more than four years of age when my mom left to go back to her home in Kenya. At that time, Nate was stable, as his last surgery had been when he was the age of two and half years. He started kindergarten when he turned five years of age.

When Nate started school, I took him to school every morning. Then I went to work, picking him up after work and staying home with him after school. Even though I was a single mother for a several years, Nathanael never took a bus to school. I was able to take him to school and pick him up because God had made provision for that before I realized I needed it. I was home with my son over the weekends. God is able to do anything that is according to His will if we trust Him. I am very thankful that I was able to spend a lot of time with Nathanael every day. This gave me the opportunity to know him very well and to understand his needs. It helped me have confidence during the times when I was faced with having to advocate for him. I was able to do a lot of studying on what I could do to help Nathanael thrive in his life. Given my son's brain condition, some of the specialists who treated him wanted to start him on various medications, such as medicine for ADHD. He was expected to have all sorts of complications, so his health care providers suggested to medicate him ahead of time. Thanks to God, I was in school as a psychology major, which equipped me to search for information related to Nathanael's health problems. I was my child's primary caregiver. My observation of how he was growing did not seem to indicate any problems. I reasoned with the medical staff. Since Nathanael was not going to day care, they decided it was okay to wait and see what happened. I did not feel that Nathanael should be put on medications to prevent symptoms of something with which he did not present. I completely respect doctors and their medical experience, but at the same time I believe that a person knows her own body, and her children's bodies, very well. Therefore, the knowledge from both patient and doctor should be considered when it comes to being treated. Some doctors made it clear that I was not their favorite parent to work with, but in the long run things worked out well for my child. To date, twelve years after it was first suggested, Nathanael has not needed ADHD medication or any other medication his doctors suggested he start taking as a baby. The only medication he has needed, when he was close to seven years old, was ant seizure medicine. At school, he has not been a problem child and is reported to be very well behaved, gentle-spirited, genuine, kind, bighearted, etc. He has never caused any trouble in class or among his friends. I had prayed many times that God would miraculously make Nathanael's brain normal. Instead, God showed me that He can work with any brain in a normal way. When Nathanael went to kindergarten, he was like the other children and was very smart in class. I know that Nathanael is a miracle because the doctors say they don't understand what makes him functions as he does.

Part Three

The Medical Journey

Nathanael has been blessed with great health apart from his brain-related problems. Apart from his routine doctor visits, he has needed a doctor on extremely rare occasions, fewer than five times in his entire life, for other illnesses, such as colds and coughs. However, he does suffered from his major brain problems. Two of the complications thereof, namely hydrocephalus and seizures, have seriously affected his life. His journey to stability has been extremely trying.

Going through this tough journey has been made much easier on me by the constant support of my family, who have come to help me out when possible and who stay connected by way of phone conversations. Another blessing has been my faithful friends like Agnes, Jennifer, Alice, Christine, Mac, and Joan, to mention a few. There are others, including people from my former workplace, Hospice of the Twin Cities. Some of my coworkers there stood with me through very tough times.

Hydrocephalus

Cerebrospinal fluid (CSF) is a clear, watery fluid that is continuously produced and absorbed in the brain. Every person has cerebrospinal fluid flowing in the ventricles of the brain, around the surface of the brain, and through the spinal cord. Cerebrospinal fluid is produced by tissues that line the ventricles of the brain. It flows through the ventricles by way of interconnecting channels, eventually flowing into spaces around the brain and the spinal column. Cerebrospinal fluid serves many functions that are important to the brain. It bathes the brain and spinal column as well as removes waste products of the brain's metabolism. It also keeps the brain buoyant, allowing the relatively heavy brain to float within the skull. CSF provides cushioning to the brain so as to prevent brain injury. It also flows back and forth between the brain cavity and spinal column to maintain a constant pressure within the brain, compensating for changes in blood pressure that may affect the brain.

In the case where there is excess cerebrospinal fluid in the ventricle of the brain, hydrocephalus occurs. Hydrocephalus is caused when the flow of fluid is blocked or when there is an imbalance between the amount of cerebrospinal fluid produced and the amount absorbed into the bloodstream. Hydrocephalus is the buildup of fluid in the ventricles deep within the brain. The excess fluid increases the size of the ventricles and puts pressure on the brain. The pressure caused by too much cerebrospinal fluid, a condition associated with hydrocephalus, can damage brain tissues and cause a large spectrum of impairments in brain function. Although hydrocephalus can happen to anyone at any age, it is more common among infants and older adults. Hydrocephalus can surgically be treated, to restore and maintain normal cerebrospinal fluid levels in the brain. A variety of interventions are often required to manage symptoms or functional impairments resulting from hydrocephalus

Nathanael happens to have an extremely complicated hydrocephalus condition. Often a shunt is placed in the brain to help drain the blocked CSF. Instead of just a single blockage in the flow of the absorption of the CSF, Nate has multiple areas in his brain where the flow was blocked and where cysts formed as a result. This makes it difficult for shunts to work successfully for him. Because of this, he has needed many brain surgeries to bring balance to the flow of cerebrospinal fluid in his brain. Eighteen of his twenty surgeries were to treat something related to his hydrocephalus (the other two surgeries were performed to try to control his seizures). Nathanael first had a shunt first in his brain when he was five days old. That surgery was followed by multiple shunt revisions. In the process of one of these shunt revisions, he has had one major shunt infection, which nearly took his life when he was about two and half years old. Otherwise, the brain surgeries were all successful. He recovered well from them all.

The Shunt Infection—One of Nate's Most Serious Fights

When Nathanael was two years old, he went through a shunt revision. About a month after that revision, he started getting very sick on a regular basis. He was vomiting several times a day, complaining of pain in his stomach. Nathanael has always been difficult to figure out, because he is a very strong-willed child with a high pain threshold. His complaints brought him to the ER multiple times. Each time we visited, the staff did CT scans on Nate and then sent us back home once the images indicated he was stable after having just had the surgery. I desperately watched him get worse with every passing day. Yet at the ER, the staff looked at me like I was crazy. Nathanael looks very good even when he is in pain. I told the staff that my son was not okay, but they did not believe me.

Two months passed by. He had lost a lot of weight, and his vomiting had gotten worse. When I took him to the ER, he wanted to play. According to the staff, he acted like a normal, healthy child. I begged and pleaded with the staff, but none of them could see what I was seeing. Even when I told them that I had taken care of this child every day of his life and that I knew he was really sick and needed help, they looked at me like I was crazy. They stated he was more nauseous than usual because of the shunt in his brain and that he would always be more nauseous than other people. I tried to reason with them, saying that he had changed a lot of late, even for a boy who has had a shunt in his brain most of his life. Nothing I said worked. Each time I took Nate to the ER, I was sent away with him, because he was active, had no fever, and was acting normal in the presence of the ER staff. The staff sent samples of Nate's blood into a lab, and the test results came back normal. I had no way of convincing the people at the ER how sick he was, but God came through.

What got the attention of the neurosurgical team was Nate's swollen belly three months into his suffering. The CT scans still indicated he was stable. In addition, he was acting normal and had no fevers, and his blood work had revealed no problem. The health care practitioners decided to do a shunt tap. This entails going directly into the head where the shunt is in place and then drawing a sample of spinal fluid from there. This was what revealed the problem: Nate had a serious shunt infection. That meant he would have to stay nearly a month in the hospital.

While Nate was in the hospital being treated for his shunt infection, he was put on four different IV antibiotics. They had to replace several IVs, which led the staff to implant a central IV for delivering the medication. Allergic to one of the antibiotics, he got even more sick when taking it. I remember my child looking me in the eye during this time and speaking to my heart: "I can't do this anymore."

I looked into his eyes and said, "You can, and you will fight." I encouraged him not to give up as I held him in my arms. I remember that he closed his eyes and said nothing as I encouraged him, but I knew he heard me. This was a child who never seemed to feel any pain, even on the day after brain surgery.

Once the staff identified the antibiotic to which Nate was allergic and then stopped administering it to him, he started to feel better. A different IV antibiotic ran for two weeks to clear all the infection from his shunt. After this, he had to have another surgery, to remove the entire shunt system and replace it with a completely new system so as to avoid any chance of infection recurring. Nate was then put on more antibiotics. Once he was stable and back to normal, he was discharged. This was one of his several prolonged hospitalizations. I thank God that of all the surgeries Nate has had, this was the only one done to treat an infection. Going through these several months was one of the most trying times for me as a newly single mother. Thankfully, my mom was with me. Her presence meant the world to me and to Nate.

Nate's Seizures

Having seizures is not a disease in and of itself. Instead, a seizure is a symptom that indicates something else. A seizure is an abnormal electrical discharge in the brain. This uncontrolled electrical activity in the brain may produce a physical convulsion, minor physical signs, thought disturbances, or a combination of symptoms. The type of symptoms and seizure depends on where the abnormal electrical activity takes place in the brain, what its cause is, and such factors as the patient's age and general state of health. Seizures can be caused by various things like head injuries, infectious illnesses, brain tumors, mal-development of the brain, and fevers, among others. While many causes of seizures have been identified, there are many times when no cause for seizures is yet found in many patients. Sometimes a person will experience warning signs before having a seizure. One of these warning signs is the affected person's experience of an aura.

An aura is a perceptual disturbance experienced by some people who suffer from migraine or seizures, before either the headache or seizure starts. It often manifests as the perception of a strange light or an unpleasant smell, or confusing thoughts or experiences. Some people experience an aura without a migraine or seizure following it. An aura is often the first sign that a seizure may happen. A person may have an aura for several seconds, for several minutes, and even up to an hour before a seizure happens. Most people who have auras have the same type of aura every time they experience one. Auras warn seizure-prone people to get to safety before the seizure happens.

Nathanael started a battle with seizures right before he turned seven years of age. Prior to that, he was not having seizures and was not on any medications. He has seen auras appear before he has a seizure, and sometimes he has had auras appear without having a seizure. Nathanael has been treated using medication, surgery, and a Ketogenic diet. By the time he was twelve, the treatments proved themselves effective.

Currently, for the first time in his entire life, Nathanael has been away from the ER and hospitals for more than about a year and half.

Struggle with Seizures—Some Dangerous Moments: An Extremely Emotionally, Mentally, Physically, and Spiritually Exhausting Battle

By the time Nathanael was about two and half, he had undergone a total of seven brain surgeries. All of these were related to the malfunctioning of his shunt system. After that, Nathanael spent five years without many complications. Still we were aware of how delicate his brain was, medically speaking. He made several ER visits and sometimes stayed overnight for observation at a hospital because of the nature of his condition, but nothing serious happened with regard to Nate's health in those five years.

Nathanael and I visited our family in Kenya two times during those five years. Our first trip was when he was about five years old. The next took place a year later, when he was about six years old. It took a lot of courage on my part to travel so far away from his doctors, but it was another opportunity for me to surrender. His doctors always gave him a checkup before we left, and they gave me instructions in case Nate had a medical emergency while we were in Kenya. Nathanael was not on any medications when we took either of our trips. Indeed the trips were wonderful, with no complications while we were in Kenya. During those trips, Nate got to connect very closely with his grandparents, aunts, uncles, and cousins, who all welcomed him in a very special way. This made him develop a very special place in his heart for his extended family as well as for Kenya.

The June after our second trip to and from Kenya brought huge challenges for Nathanael and me. It was the first week of June when something very strange happened, something that was completely unexpected, because Nathanael had been doing so well for such a long time. Having already finished getting Nathanael ready for school, I was in the kitchen preparing breakfast. Nathanael was watching a kids' show on TV while he waited to eat. All of a sudden, I heard an extremely loud scream come from him. As I was running toward him, I noticed that he was moving his hands as if he were fighting something. His head was turned toward the left. I had no idea what was happening to him. I ran and then gathered him into my arms, going down on my knees to hold him better. All of a sudden, he started shaking and twitching. I held him, called to him, cried, and then started screaming for help. At that moment, I thought Nate was dying. I was in a state of shock and disbelief as I pleaded desperately to God for help. Nate's twitching movements eventually stopped. He looked at me, appearing very scared. At that moment, I placed him down on the floor and said, "I've got to call 9-1-1." I grabbed my phone from the table and then returned to Nate to hold him. He appeared very tired, and he was unable to talk. I called 9-1-1. The dispatcher who answered my call stayed on the phone with me, asking me what Nate was doing and giving me instructions until the paramedics arrived.

I had managed to calm down somewhat, especially after I saw my son look me in the eyes and I discerned that he was breathing. Once the paramedics arrived, they checked him out and took his medical history. I did not know what had happened to my son. I could only describe to the paramedics what I had heard and seen. Nathanael, though his speech was slurred after this episode, was now able to talk, so he told the paramedics what he had seen that had made him scream so loud. He said that he had seen a big red balloon that looked like a crown coming toward him. He mentioned that it was very scary. He fell deep asleep shortly after telling them that.

The paramedics then asked me if Nate had a history of seizures. I replied that I had never seen him have one before. They stated their belief about what had just happened: that Nate had had a seizure. I rode in the ambulance as Nate was transported to the ER. Because of his medical history with hydrocephalus, he was taken to an examination room right away. Once the doctors started checking him out, he got up and began acting completely normal, telling the story of what had happened to him as he remembered it. His speech was back to normal, and he could walk as usual. I was still in shock, confused about what I had seen that morning. Little did I know that it was a start of a new struggle.

During this ER visit, Nate was subjected to CT scans and X-rays of his shunt system. Those tests indicated he was stable. After he was kept for observation in the ER, he was discharged with instructions to follow up with the neurologist he had once seen when he was a year old.

Nathanael saw the neurologist, who decided to do imaging to determine whether Nate's brain had undergone significant changes. I did not want Nathanael to be put on medications without the doctor's first figuring out what was happening to him. Nate ended up having another seizure a month later, and then one in the week following that. At that time, his doctor had determined that he needed another surgery to revise the shunt. After that surgery was done, Nate's seizures disappeared. At the same time, Nate was having allergic reactions to the anticonvulsants he had been started on. Since his body was reacting negatively to the medication, I requested that he be taken off the medication. Doing this would show if the shunt revision had stopped Nathan from having seizures. Deep inside my heart, I knew that medication was not the answer for Nathanael. Nathanael's body does not do well with medications.

During a short time on a new ant seizure medication, Nate became disoriented and his functioning slowed. After he had gone for six months without taking that medication, he stopped having seizures. At this time, however, he had another seizure, one that was serious. Thankfully, his neurologist found an anticonvulsive that worked without causing an allergic reaction.

As I've already mentioned, imaging test results showed that Nathanael needed another shunt revision. Unfortunately, his neurologist did not have a contract for practicing at the hospital of which Nathanael was a patient at that time. Nathanael started being seen by a doctor who was part of the neurology department that did contract with this hospital. This neurology department was very different in its operation from the one to which Nate previously went for his appointments.

This was another difficult period, as Nathanael spent many days in ERs, being admitted to and then discharged from the hospital time and again. Given how often they answered my calls about my son, the paramedics got to know Nathanael.

The confusing thing about Nathanael's condition was that there was always a worry about the hydrocephalus in his brain. Therefore, any symptoms he had that might indicate a problem with hydrocephalus, including seizures, landed him in the hospital. His body has been subjected to more radiation than I'm comfortable with.

Nate's Struggle with Medications

Nathanael was seven years old when he went through two brain surgeries to revise his shunt. He was having seizure after seizure, and was in the ER every other day. He had three seizures a day on several days in spite of his being on a medication. The imaging showed yet again that there was pressure on Nathanael's brain, a complication of his hydrocephalus. I felt that my son's new neurologists quickly wrote him off because of his brain condition. These doctors were avoiding subjecting Nate to more surgeries. Instead of operating on him, they increased the dose of his anticonvulsive medication.

Nathanael continued to have seizures, but these seizures were prolonged. He also became disoriented, a side effect of the high dose of medication. His seizures became worse. He was admitted to the hospital for observation. Even when the imaging clearly showed that there was too much pressure on Nathanael's brain, his neurologists would not consider doing surgery on him. I watched my child go through another difficult time of suffering. And I was a single mother going through this period, with no family around to lean on. Most of my friends had gotten tired of running back and forth to support me and Nate in the hospital. They had moved on. I was struggling to hold onto my job because even though my company was supportive, I was always aware work has to get done and afraid they might get tired of me, with my running back and forth to the hospital. Although life was normally tough for Nathanael and me compared to most other people's lives, this was an especially tough period of our lives. Thankfully, when things became too tough, my father came from Kenya and helped me out for six months. After that, he returned to Kenya.

Within the time my father was helping me, my son's seizures got worse even with the neurologists increasing his anti seizure medications again and again. His health care team pushed to start him on a different medications. I pleaded with them not to put him on that medicine. In raising Nathanael, I've found that he does not tolerate medications well, as I've mentioned previously. Simple medications like those for colds and coughs only make him sicker. His previous neurologist had trialed different anti seizure medications before finding one that did not cause allergic reaction. In spite of my efforts to explain that Nathanael reacts poorly to medications, this group of neurologists put Nathanael on one medication after another. He became more and more sick. I watched the doctors have divided opinions about Nathanael's condition. He continued to suffer while under their care. He was having seizure, followed by vomiting and headache multiple times within a day. This was really scary for me to watch. I had never felt as desperate in my life as I felt during this time. These neurologists were very cold and disrespectful toward me. The way some of them looked at me while I was discussing my observations of my child was very demeaning. Some looked at me like I was the stupidest human being they had ever seen. I did not see a single shred of concern in their eyes. What saddened my heart more was that I saw they held the same attitude toward Nathanael. They all got mad at me for not saying yes to whatever they wanted to do with my child. I was wasting their time, they said, because they already knew about my child's condition. They kept reminding me of how much experience they had from working with people who had this type of condition. Nothing I said made an impact on them. Nothing! Anytime I opened my mouth to speak of hope, they reminded me how bad my child's brain condition was and said that I should accept it. I pleaded with them, asking them to see Nate as a normally functioning child, and they told me I was lucky that he functioned at all. They told me I was in denial of my child's condition, saying that what he needed was medication.

I remember one particular day during this period. I was crying and pleading with one of these neurologists, asking him to schedule surgery for Nathanael. I will never forget his posture and the look in his eyes as I was talking. He looked at me from head to toe, and again from head to toe, before he turned and then left the room. I felt like a knife had gone through my heart.

When not having seizures or vomiting, Nathanael often climbed out of his hospital bed. Nathanael suffered emotionally as well due to all the suffering he was enduring. He was so tired. His neurologists told me that they wanted to prescribe a medication to stop this behavior. I, however, did not want my child to take more medicine. The conviction in my heart said that there was more to life for Nathanael than what I could see with my eyes. I refused any additional medications. When the neurologists fought my decision, I called the hospital's administration department.

I felt that things began to go much better once the hospital administrators were involved. The unit doctors at the hospital, who were very sympathetic and supportive, fought hard for Nathanael on my behalf. It was helpful that the team on the unit that watched what was happening with Nathanael every day fought on our behalf. Some of these doctors had known Nathanael from previous hospitalizations and could see the difference in him. After Nate had spent at least two weeks in the hospital suffering greatly, the team of neurologists with whom I was unhappy were taken off Nate's case. I refused the neurology department any further contact with Nathanael. Nate, a week later, had a double surgery which left Nate back to his normal. I asked the hospital that my child be followed by his former neurologist even though that doctor did not contract with this hospital.

Later and with God's help, I was able to forgive of the pain and misery that the team of neurologists had caused my child. I now tell my story about this experience because I know many people go through similar experiences. The fact that one group of doctors did not work out for Nathanael did not mean that no doctor could. I did not understand why that team of neurologists were the way they were. In my experience with Nathanael, who has been hospitalized a great deal, I have never had anything close to the experience I had with that team of neurologists. I can understand their plight, and that of any doctor struggling with what to do for Nathanael, because my son's condition is very complex. What I cannot wrap my mind around is how insensitive they were about Nathanael's long-term suffering. I also have trouble understanding how those neurologists could have been as cold as they were, disregarding me as a mother. Their behavior is one of the things I have had to forgive and hand over to God.

Nathanael was discharged from the hospital after nearly a month and recovered well from the surgeries. For that time, He'd had no seizures and no vomiting, and his behavior was back to his norm. I had contacted his earlier neurologist who continued Nate's care and I was able to release my father so he could go back to his home in Kenya.

Nate was nine years old when he started having seizures again. He ended up having another surgery to revise his shunt, but that did not help with the seizures. His surgeon at the time, suggested talking with the neurologist to see if he could do something more for Nathanael. At that moment, I felt like the children of Israel facing the Red Sea, their enemies behind them. I could not imagine going down the road of increasing medications again. But all along, I had a strong feeling in my heart that something could be done for Nathanael. I never felt hopeless, although I had no idea what could be done. Little did I know that Nate's lack of tolerance for medication would lead to findings and decisions that would eventually work out for Nate. That is how mysteriously God works.

The Darkest Days of the Darkest Period

During this chaotic period of my single motherhood, I found myself pregnant from a man I trusted, never mind that he and I had broken up several times. If you are wondering what I was thinking, I can assure you that I was not thinking at all. I was merely surviving, seeking whatever support I could get. Once I announced to this man that I was pregnant, he abandoned me. There I was, pregnant and without a husband. My father had just come from Kenya when I found out I was pregnant. As hard as it was, I told him that I was pregnant and had been abandoned by the child's father. My father was shocked when I imparted this news, but he was supportive of me.

Nathanael was going through an extremely tough time. I was still working at holding onto my job. I am thankful to God that I had my dad to lean on. Many people whom I had known deserted me and talked about me very negatively. I had two faithful friends who stuck with me though. A few other friends did not exit my life at that time, but I don't believe they had any idea what I was facing. My workplace and my coworkers were completely God-sent.

Being a spiritual-care provider and an ordained minister did not make my life any easier. I was a divorced woman, I had a child, I was pregnant, and I had been abandoned by the latter child's father. Many people lost trust in me and treated me horribly. I was mocked during this period of my life.

My father went back to Kenya after Nate had had surgery and seemed to be stable. I was pregnant but was coping just fine when Dad left. For some time after I had found out I was pregnant, I was in a bad place emotionally. There were other things going on in my life, too: spending sleepless nights in the hospital; racing to and from the hospital; struggling with neurologists who did not seem to care a bit for my child; and seeing people go out of my life. The pregnancy, however, was a happy thing for me even though I did not expect to be abandoned.

Once Nate settled a bit, I had time to think about my life and to realize I was carrying another life in my body, one that deserved the best. With God's help, I made some conscious decisions in regard to my life and my children. I prayed to God for forgiveness, and God gave me peace. From that moment on, it was easier for me to deal with those who mocked me or laughed at me, because the only One who really counts, God the Father was with me. My friends Agnes and Christine helped me with Nathanael when I needed help after my father went back to Kenya. They also came to my apartment many times and helped me clean up and do laundry when I couldn't. They never got tired of my chaos and I will cherish them forever, as their friendship meant a great deal to me during that period of my life.

Also, I was very blessed with a pretty flexible work schedule that enabled me to spend a lot of time with Nathanael. I therefore got to know Nathanael so well that I could easily detect any slight change in his condition. I knew when he was not feeling himself. I would say that out of the many times he has been sick and had seizures, I was with him for at least 95 percent of those. On the days I noticed he was not okay, I stayed with him. Sure enough, my instinct was right almost every time. However, the worst thing of all happened to Nathanael while I was pregnant with my beautiful daughter: he literally quit breathing while I was at work.

On that ordinary morning, I got up as usual and prepared Nathanael for the day. He had been doing well for several months. On this particular morning, he looked great. As previously mentioned, I was pregnant with my daughter, Sally, at this time. Though this period was generally stressful for me, I had made up my mind to focus on the important things in my life. Carrying my daughter inside my body was one of them. I had made a conscious decision that I would not pass stress onto my unborn baby, who had no say in the circumstances of my life. I was coping well. Nathanael's school was closed for summer. It would be nearly two months before Sally was born. It was a happy and peaceful time of my life. I dropped Nathanael at my friend Christine's on my way to work. Christine often helped me out. She happened to be with Agnes's sons, Matthew and Osteen, with whom Nathanael had grown up. Agnes and I sometimes cared for each other's children, which caused our children to grow very close to one another. Christine, a kindhearted soul, helped Agnes and me out on many occasions even though she did not have children of her own.

On this day, Nate, Matthew, and Osteen were playing as usual. Although Christine had watched Nathanael for me many times before, she had never witnessed him having a seizure—that is, not until this morning. It took her a few moments to notice what was going on. Nathanael all of a sudden stopped playing. He walked across the room to the couch and sat down. He was not talking. Around that time, I called Christine to check in on Nathanael. She handed him the phone. I talked to him, and he responded with few words. I thought he was distracted, playing with his friends, so I said good-bye to him and then hung up the phone.

I had a home care appointment with a patient of Hospice of the Twin Cities to provide spiritual support. As soon as I had said hello to this patient, my phone rang. Seeing it was Christine calling, I answered. Right away, Christine said, "Nathanael is having a seizure. What do I do?!" I could tell she was in panic mode. I stayed calm and stepped out of the patient's house to ask Christine if Nathanael was safe. She said he was still on the couch. I told her to call 9-1-1, asking her to have the paramedics call me once they got to her place. I told her what to do in the meantime.

God has blessed me with calmness, especially in tough times. The person I was visiting, and that person's family, had no idea what had happened. I stepped back into the house and informed them that I had to leave because there was an emergency. I believe they thought it was work-related, since I worked with people who were at the end of life. I called my supervisor to let her know what was happening as I drove off. I have never driven so fast in my life—and without thinking that there might be police on the road. A paramedic called me and was asking me questions as I approached Christine's place, but he did not tell me what was going on with my son.

On arrival, I found more people than I had ever seen in all the times I had called 9-1-1, including firefighters. I panicked when I saw all these people surrounding the ambulance that Nathanael was inside. I walked right through the crowd with my big tummy, asking what was happening. One of the people held me and stated, "He is not breathing. We are putting a tube in his windpipe so he can breathe." I felt dizzy, like I was going to pass out. For a moment, everything was too much for me to digest. All I wanted to do was to get close to my son and hold him, but people held me back.

Once the paramedics had put tube was in place, I pleaded to get close to my son. Someone led me to him in the back of the ambulance. I held Nate's hand and talked to him as the driver drove the ambulance to the closest hospital. Nate roused slightly once we arrived at the hospital. On the way to the hospital, a paramedic had told me that Nathanael had had a forty-five-minute seizure. The paramedics had administered Versed to stop the seizure, and Nathanael quit breathing after that. Of all the seizures Nathanael has had, he had never had one of this magnitude. He usually had one- to three-minute seizures. On occasion, his seizure lasted between five and eight minutes. He was on anticonvulsants when this one occurred. When Nate aroused, he was worn out from the seizure and had complained of pain in his throat. He could hardly speak as had lost his voice from the intubation. He was confused and appeared to be afraid not knowing what had happened to him. I thank God for enabling me to be right beside him because I was the only thing that he recognized and gave him comfort.

Now at the hospital, Nate was stable enough to be transported. He was soon transferred to his regular hospital. He was observed for a period of time and then was discharged. I believe the effect this day hard on me got Sally born prematurely two weeks later through an emergency C-section.

God's grace is sufficient. Nathanael was okay for the next two weeks. When I ended up in the hospital unexpectedly to have Sally, my friend Agnes kept Nathanael for me. I had no strength to spend on worry, so I surrendered it all to God. Nathanael had no health problems while I was in the hospital. Agnes brought him in to the hospital every day so he could spend some time with his sister and me. I was very sick when I was discharged.

I believe that God makes messages of our messes in the most mysterious of ways. Sally weighed about two pounds when she was born. She stayed in the NICU for two weeks after her birth. Once discharged, she weighed about three pounds. The two weeks she was kept in the NICU gave me time to recover enough for her to come home. Nathanael wanted to be with me as soon as I got home. While in the hospital, I had prayed every day that God would intervene for me—and He did. And for the next two months, Nathanael was okay. Thereafter, he had multiple seizures. This happened during the time I had been told that Nathanael was not a candidate for surgery.

My Search for More

There I was with my child having increased seizures even though he was on an anti-seizure medication that had worked for him without allergic reaction. As I prayed, I felt my heart leading me to search the Internet to see what I could find. Nathanael was having seizures several times a day, accompanied by headaches and vomiting. I scheduled an urgent appointment with his neurologist at the time Dr. Brenningstell, (who was very sensitive and caring and I trusted). He decided to increase his medication to see that would help while we waited for the appointment date, but it didn't help.

Nathanael struggled greatly with having seizures because his seizures were partial and started with auras. Even though he would get confused, he was aware to a great extent which made him feel very helpless and scared. By this time, I had become comfortable with handling my son's seizures, although they were never a good experience. I felt my heart sink each time he had a seizure, but I had to stay strong for his sake. I held my child in my arms and prayed, comforting him through each of his seizures. Many times, he recited the Twenty-Third Psalm, which he had known by heart since he was six years old. He would call for help and start praying once he realized the onset of the seizures until he couldn't any more. He would hold tightly onto me or anyone close to him very afraid.

As we waited for Nate's scheduled appointment, I searched the Internet. I found out there are brain surgeries specifically to help reduce or eliminate seizures. I believe that God had led me to find this information. None of Nate's doctors had told me there was such an option, because they did not believe Nathanael to be a candidate for such a major brain surgery. When I went to the appointment, I asked the neurologist about this finding. He talked to me about the procedure, informing me that it had been ruled out as too risky for Nathanael. I reasoned with Nathanael's neurologist. The medications were having a negative effect on my son. At the age of seven, Nate was at a point of barely being able to walk, losing his bowel control, losing his teeth after falling, becoming disoriented, etc. I felt strongly that we needed to take a risk if he were to survive. Maybe this type of brain surgery might cripple him or kill him. But the medications were sure crippling him and might have killed him eventually. I thank God for this neurologist, Dr. Brenningstell, for his love for Nathanael, and for his understanding. He referred Nathanael to what he referred to as "a terrific neurologist" at the Mayo Clinic. The Mayo Clinic is known for its great success in treating complicated diseases as well as medical complications.

Nathanael was scheduled for an appointment. Once we were at the Mayo Clinic, I met his new neurologist, who was sent from above. On the first appointment, she collected as much information from me as possible. I have few words to describe this new neurologist. Full of compassion and care, she listened with her heart. I had never felt so heard as I felt on the day I met Dr. Nickels. Having had already received Nate's medical record along with copies of the images sent from all his previous places of treatment, she had reviewed this information. During this appointment, I felt that Dr. Nickels had taken the time to completely understand where I was coming from. I got the sense that she knew what the most important things were concerning my child. She was not focused on how his brain images appeared. She was impressed to see how well he functioned, wanting him to continue functioning at that level. She was completely holistic in her approach. In talking with me, she did not appear to be looking down on me. As she sat on her chair, I could feel the embrace of care from her heart. She listened, very patiently and carefully, to everything I said—and I had a lot to say. Throughout that lengthy appointment, she was completely engaged. She heard my heart's cry for my child. She felt me with a mother's heart. As I left that appointment that day, I felt a peace I had not felt at any other point of Nate's treatment journey. I felt that Dr. Nickels had been sent directly to save my child's life. She seemed to understand with her heart

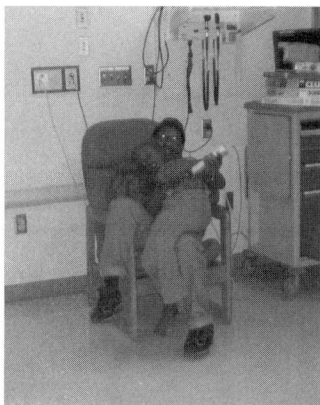

Nate at seven years
old, with Grandpa

Eight-year-old Nate; Sally at a few
months old; and their mom

Nate the big brother

A single mother of two. When she
is not at the hospital, life goes on.

At the Mayo Clinic

Hope Was on Its Way

Nathanael went through about six months of testing to see if he qualified to have brain surgery to help with his seizures. The Mayo Clinic was two and half drive, one way from our residence, so fuel for the long drives was a significant expense. On many occasions Nathanael had a seizure on our way to the hospital or on our way back home. Other times he had seizures while we were waiting to be seen at the hospital. I always dreaded the appointment days and what the journey was going to be like. It is one thing to have your child having seizures when he is at home or near home; it is another thing for him to have seizures when he is in a car, away from home. Many times Nate vomited in the car, either after or before he had a seizure, but we had to continue our journey anyway. Still, I was feeling very encouraged that Nathanael was in good hands at the Mayo Clinic. He was admitted a number of times, three days each time, in the monitoring unit to locate which part of his brain was causing the seizures. Thanks to God and a dedicated team of professionals, the latter located the place in Nate's brain that was causing the seizures.

My heart holds a very special place for Nathanael's neurologist Dr. Nickels, who saw Nathanael past his brain condition and for the potential God had placed in him. Most of all, I am thankful to God for the ways in which He works.

The scheduled surgery was risky for Nathanael. At the same time, he had medication allergies. I believe that if Nathanael's body hadn't been allergic to medications, this surgery would have been ruled out for him. He would have been fed medications if his body tolerated them, and he would not have been the Nathanael I know today. God had it all figured out before I had come close to seeing what was happening.

I first noticed that Nathanael had medication allergies when he had had bad reactions to cough and cold medications, long before he needed to be on seizure medications. All along, ever since Nathanael had started having seizures, I begged his doctors to do surgery to stop the seizures. I had no clue there was such a surgery. My observation was that of all the fifteen shunt-revision surgeries Nathanael had, he recovered from them quickly and with no side effects. But all the medication his doctors put him on left him in a worse condition and nearly killed him. My heart was very confident about this surgery, although I had no understanding of the procedure at the time. I believe that God worked things out this way and was showing me something in my spirit.

The new team of doctors were concerned about Nathanael's delicate brain, but they approved focal cortical resection surgery because his body was not tolerating medications well. That was one of my happiest days. When I studied this surgery, I felt very strongly that Nathanael had nothing to lose by going through it. He did have everything to gain if he survived it. My heart was ready, surrendered to God.

Nate and I met his new surgeon, Dr. Wetjen, at the Mayo Clinic. After talking with Dr. Wetjen, I felt like this was meant to be. God had brought Nathanael to a place of hope. God had heard the cries of our hearts. Nathanael and I had prayed for what felt like a million years. Many times, I held my child as he cried, asking me why God was not healing him in spite of all our prayers. I did not know the answer, but I told him that we must continue to trust God no matter what life brings. I talked to him about the many times when God had come through for us. I encouraged him to stay focused on giving thanks to God for the many things God had done for us. Many times when he felt the auras and as a seizure manifested, Nate started reciting the Twenty-Third Psalm. We kept praying and trusting.

Dr. Wetjen viewed life from the eyes of God. He did not like the fact that Nathanael had seizures. He talked to us about the surgery, mentioning that he had confidence that it was going to benefit Nathanael and give him a better life than the life he was living. He didn't minimize what could happen during the surgery, however. This surgeon simply had complete faith, which was comforting for me and my son. He said without hesitation that he was going to perform the focal cortical resection, because he felt it was in Nate's best interest. I left Dr. Wetjen's office feeling confident that Nathanael was on his way to victory.

In spite of my family's crazy life, I had made up my mind a long time ago that we were going to live life. I did whatever I could to give Nathanael a normal life. I decided not just to sit around and wait for when Nathanael got sick. Instead, I made up my mind that we would keep living. And when Nathanael got sick, we would stop for that moment before we continued living.

I became okay with the fact that my plans were interrupted and changed almost on a daily basis, sometimes hour to hour. I gave control to God and gave Him my hand. At the time when Nathanael started the testing at the Mayo Clinic, we had planned to visit Kenya and had our passports ready. I had a daughter by this time, whom my family had not met. I had also gotten remarried, and my family in Kenya had not yet met my husband. For Nathanael, it was going to be another trip to Kenya, although a very different one. The previous times he went to Kenya, he was not having seizures and was not on any medication. This time, things were different, and we were okay with that. However, we ended up canceling our trip to Kenya. Nathanael's surgery was scheduled for right about the time we were planning on traveling; he had to be the first priority. It was disappointing to all of us at first, but once we put everything into perspective, we saw that there could not have been a better plan than to have Nathanael's procedure done when his doctors were ready to do it. The surgery was going to be done in two parts: brain mapping followed by focal cortical resection.

Summary of treatment at Mayo Clinic

SUMMARY OF NATE'S EPILEPSY SURGERY AT MAYO
FORWARDED BY DR. NICKELS.

Question 1: can we find the area of seizure onset?

Plan: 1) MRI of head with special sequences that allow better imagining for the patients with epilepsy
2) Admit to pediatric Epilepsy monitoring unit to record seizures and see if the EEG placed on his scalp showed abnormal electrical activity over just a small area of his brain, a larger region of his brain or the whole right side of his brain.

Results: 1) MRI
The MRI showed Nate's brain malformations were actually worse than previously thought. Not only does Nate have a complicated hydrocephalus with cysts of cerebrospinal fluid, but he also has multiple large areas on the right where the outer part of the brain (the cortex, or grey matter) did not form correctly. The connection between the two sides did not form correctly. The coordination

part of the brain (cerebellum) also did not form correctly. There was also concern there may be some subtle abnormalities in the formation of the left hemisphere, although this wasn't clear.

2) EEG

In between seizures, there were frequent brief bursts of abnormal electrical activity throughout the right side, as would be expected for the extent of structural abnormalities. Fortunately, the seizures showed a pretty focal onset over the right parietal region.

Question 2: Can we operate?

Given the extensive abnormalities on the right, most people would look at modified hemispherectomy (disconnecting the entire right side of the brain) or complete hemispherectomy (actually removing the entire right side of the brain). The problem is that this leaves kids paralyzed on one side (the left for Nate), so we only do it if there is already considerable weakness that wouldn't be significantly worsened by surgery. This was not the case for Nate. He had only slight weakness on the left when I first saw him. Sometimes, when kids are born with a very abnormal hemisphere, the good hemisphere takes over essentially all of the functions from the bad side-including motor control. This is why we tried to have Nate do functional MRI-It would have shown us if it was actually the left side of Nate's brain that was providing motor control over both the left and the right body. Unfortunately, Nate was too young to be able to do this test, so hemisphertomy/hemispherectomy was not an option for Nate. We were back to tried to get a better idea if there was just a small part of Nate's brain that was causing the seizures, even though it looked like they could be coming from anywhere on the right. Since hemispherectomy wasn't an option, I was hoping we could find a smaller area the surgeon could remove while leaving in the brain that controls motor.

Back to Question 1: Can we find the seizure onset zone?

We brought Nate back to the epilepsy monitoring unit to record another seizure. This time, we wanted to inject him with a special dye right during the seizure that shows the area of the brain with the highest metabolic activity during the seizure (called an ictal SPECT scan). We compare this to a baseline scan without seizures (interictal SPECT scan). By subtracting the baseline from the seizure scan, it gives us an idea of the area of the brain that has the highest metabolic activity just during the seizure, which should correspond to the seizure onset zone. Since this comes out looking like a fuzzy blob, These images are overlaid (coregistered) to his MRI. This whole process is called SISCOM (Subtraction Ictal SPECT CO-registered to MRI). Nate's EEG during that seizure, also looked like it was involving the right parietal region, which was good. The SISCOM looked like there was a pretty big active area surrounding one of his cysts in a similar region to the EEG abnormalities and both were away from the motor control area. This was helpful, but did not give us enough information to really feel confident we had found the seizure onset zone and to know for sure it didn't overlap with the motor control area of the brain.

Now what??

If we can determine the area of seizure onset down to a specific region of the brain, the next step is to record seizures with the EEG placed directly over the brain. When we record seizures with scalp EEG, the electrical activity has to go through the cerebral fluid, the brain coverings, the skull, and the skin, so some information is lost. This does require surgery and is certainly an invasive test.

In Nate's first epilepsy surgery, a small area of the skull was removed and a small plastic sheet electrodes was laid over the brain. They didn't go into the brain. Since this sheet of electrodes takes up space and the brain is very sensitive to being too crowded within the skull, we leave the bone off, but still close the brain coverings and the skin. It's essentially like Nate had a soft spot (like babies have on their heads) again. His head was then wrapped securely to keep out infection. He was then sent to ICU. While we wait for seizures to happen, all kids stay in the ICU just like Nate did. Fortunately, as was the case for Nate, kids tolerate this very well. They wake up, eat, read etc. Like with Nate, they usually stay in bed the whole time-and this can certainly take days for seizures to happen. Nate was monitored for 16 days! Nate tolerated this really well and spent most of his time happily playing video games, reading, and working on his homework. During that time, we were able to record seizures that came from the right parietal region, which was great!

Back to question 2: can we operate?

Now that we were able to confirm that the seizures really were coming from just part of Nate's brain and not the whole right side, we needed to find out if this area overlapped with the motor control part. This is why he had the test in which we stimulated the electrodes to find the area that controlled motor. He did really well with this and it was pretty much as you described. Fortunately, the motor control area did not overlap with the seizure onset zone, so we could operate!

Question 3: What type of operation?

While Nate was being monitored, the small area of skull over the electrodes was off the whole time. This meant there was essentially no pressure on his hydrocephalus. The seizures during that time were less frequent and less severe than what was he was having at home. This is why we had to record for so long to get seizures. You had always felt that his seizures would get better if we were able to find a better way to control his hydrocephalus that just putting shunt after shunt, as had been done his whole life. We decided the best option for Nate would be not only remove the area that we felt was where the seizures were coming from, but also to do more extensive surgery for his hydrocephalus. This is what Dr. Wetjen did. Nate had a focal cortical resection, but then Dr. Wetjen also went through and opened up all the cysts of fluid so that the fluid in Nate's ventricles could flow better. This was a big surgery which is why it took Nate longer to recover.

After surgery

1. We don't know for sure why Nate had a prolonged seizure from the other side. We know there is some concern that the left didn't form completely normally, so that may be part of it. We also know there is some swelling and overall irritability of the brain after a big surgery like Nate's. It was probably the combination of these.

2. Since Nate had just a focal cortical resection, it means there is still a lot of abnormal brain left that can cause seizures. This is why he still had some seizures after the surgery, even though we took out the area that was causing most of them. This is why Nate was treated with the Ketogenic diet.

3. Nate had another hydrocephalus surgery about 1.5 year later. This surgery not only replaced his shunt, but further opened up those cysts so that fluid could flow better. I suspect it has been the combination of the hydrocephalus

surgeries and the Ketogenic diet that has allowed Nate to recover from seizures.

By Dr. Katherine C. Nickels M.D. Child and Adolescent Neurology Mayo Clinic.

Brain Mapping and Focal Cortical Resection Surgery: The "No Choice but to Surrender" Moment

Here I was at last, faced with absolutely no choice but to look upwards. Nathanael was nine years old, miserable because of his seizures and faced with a life-or-death decision. The day had come when I actually had to hand my son over to his surgeon, Dr. Wetjen, at the Mayo Clinic. From all of the studies the staff had done on Nathanael's brain, they discovered that the part of his brain causing him seizures was close to the part of his brain that controlled his motor function, which was why they did not perform Hemispherectomy. (to take out one entire side of his brain). The team choose to perform the Focal Cortical Resection to avoid getting him paralyzed.

Here Nathanael, our family were knowing this but realizing that if Nathanael was going to be helped, this may have been the only way, unless God performed a miracle and provided him with a new brain. This was a time when I had to hold to the word God had given me about Nathanael before he was born. God had already shown me His faithfulness in my son's life. I felt that my only option was to trust Him all the way, even if I didn't understand. I know that God understands everything and has it all figured out. Prior to Nate's surgery, I had gathered my worship music and warfare music like I always did. I got ready to be focused totally on God, knowing how difficult this period was going to be. Thanks be to God, He had blessed me with a husband to stand beside me while my son went through this experience. Nathanael had gone through at least fifteen brain surgeries, but this one presented a greater risk than any of the others.

Most Great Things Don't Come Easy

> The Lord is my shepherd; I shall not want. He makes me lie down in green pastures. He leads me beside still waters. He restores my soul. He leads me in paths of righteousness for his name's sake. Even though I walk through the valley of the shadow of death, I will fear no evil, for thou art with me; your rod and your staff, they comfort me You prepare a table before me in the presence of my enemies; you anoint my head with oil; my cup overflows. Surely goodness and mercy shall follow me all the days of my life, and I shall dwell in the house of the Lord forever. (Psalm 23 ESV)

The long-awaited day had come. My heart was filled with emotions that I could not express. Starting on this day, there was going to be a big change in Nathanael's life! The amazing thing is that my heart was at peace in spite of the risks involved. My mind kept flashing back to how far God had brought Nate and to His promise for this child's life. I knew that God was in control, although I did not like going through the experience.

On that morning, Nathanael, Steve and I arrived at the Mayo Clinic early as scheduled and stayed with Nathanael during the preparations for his surgery. As with all the other surgeries, we prayed over Nathanael and anointed him with oil for healing, according to God's Word. Nathanael recited the Twenty-Third Psalm as my husband and I recited it along with him. This day was tough, because, at age nine, Nate was old enough to understand what surgery meant and he was more scared than he had been before the surgeries he'd had when he was younger. That made it hard for me. Thoughts of fear came rushing through my mind. I found myself wondering if this would be the last time I saw my child. For a moment, I felt like my knees were caving in. I kissed Nate's forehead once the team of doctors prepared to take him away. He looked straight into my eyes like he always did before surgery. I showed him courage. I looked right into his eyes and assured him that he was in good hands and was going to be okay. I also told him not to be afraid, as we were trusting God to see him through. I reminded him to recite the Twenty-Third Psalm in his heart when he felt afraid. Prayer and Scripture always bring a calm to Nathanael.

I will forever be thankful for divine connections. Knowing how difficult this procedure was going to be and how long Nate was going to be in the hospital, I needed help with my daughter, Sally, who was close to two years old. It was very difficult to imagine going a day without seeing her. However, I knew it would be wrong to keep her with me at the hospital this time, knowing how complicated this surgery was going to be. I had prayed ahead of time, and God placed in my heart the names of the couple I should ask for help: my friend Jennifer and her husband, John. I had seen how they raised their own children. I have a lot of respect for them as parents. Steve and I asked them if they would keep my baby daughter for at least three weeks, maybe more. They agreed wholeheartedly. They kept not only Sally but also my adopted son Morris. Steve and I were honored and touched by Jennifer and John's generosity. My daughter was very happy at their home. She had Morris as well as Jennifer's children around her.

Steve was with me the whole day. We waited for many hours after Nathanael had been taken to the operating room. It was a tough wait. Steve did a great job of supporting me and staying strong for himself, being as he was also close to Nate. We next saw Nate after almost ten hours. He looked very different.

Back from Initial Surgery

As soon as my husband and I got to Nate's recovery room, I turned on the songs that I felt ministered to me. These songs, among other worship music, were what I played over and over for the entire month that my son was recovering from this surgery. The songs that I listened to were "My God Is a Big God," "No Limits (Breakthrough)," and "Till The Walls Fall," all by Martha Munizzi.

In order to do further tests, Dr. Wetjen had cut out a piece of Nate's skull during the surgery. That sample was then frozen. Can you imagine a piece of your body staying in a freezer for sixteen days and then being put back into your body? I had never heard of such a thing! Nate's head, although wrapped, looked scary without the skull, as the skull is what gives shape to the head. Nate had grids directly placed on his brain and hanging out of his head. When I saw his head without the wrap while they changed it, it looked like intestines in a plastic bag! Scary! Thankfully, not everyone had to see that. But I could see that what I was dealing with here was different from anything I had ever seen. Nathanael's movement was limited to decrease changes of brain damage because part of his had no skull to protect it. It was sad to see Nate this way, although his attitude about it was good. He moved in bed with help and did not complain. Thanks to God, Nathanael is one of the most compliant kids you will ever know.

Once you explain something to him and he comes to understand why something is expected of him, you don't have to worry about him. He takes good care of himself, which has made life so much easier for me as a mother as well as for any person who has taken care of him.

Nate was on that hospital bed for sixteen days. In this period of time, the grids placed on his brain were hooked to a computer that was aimed at pinpointing exactly what part of the brain was causing him seizures. I was scared to death at the thought of those grids accidentally being pulled out. Out of my entire time of raising Nate, these sixteen days were the most stressful. I ached emotionally when I saw him on that bed day after day. What was even more heavy to deal with was the fear of what could happen within a split of a second if anything went wrong. He was hooked to so many machines. I could not stand to see anything above his head, no matter how stable such an object appeared to be. I held my heart in my hands the entire time. I could not sleep. I felt paralyzed for those sixteen days. By the end of it, I was in the worst emotional place of my entire life. I was thinking of my daughter, Sally, who was not used to being away from her mom. I was weak, I was exhausted, and I felt sick. I also had to work hard at putting on a brave face for my son, who frequently looks into my eyes to see what I am thinking. Anytime I show a little fear, I see his spirit crash with fear. When I show courage, he stays in very good spirits and is peaceful. Putting on a brave face was tough for me.

During the two weeks of Nate's hospitalization, I was able to go see my daughter a couple of times. Jennifer and John brought her a few times to see Nathanael. Doing so was very kind of them, seeing as their home is a three-hour drive each way from the Mayo Clinic.

Cortical Stimulation

Once the neurologists at the Mayo Clinic had located the part of the brain causing Nate's seizures, they had to figure out how that part of his brain functioned. Thankfully, they let me and my husband be there when they figured this out. It was one of the most amazing things I have ever seen. Using a computer, a tech stimulated the grids placed on Nate's head, which caused different parts of his body to move without his help. At first Nathanael was in shock. He tried to resist his moving head. I remember him saying, "What's happening? My head is moving and I am not moving it." I don't think it made any sense to him when the team explained to him what was happening. He did not like this process one bit. I can only imagine how out of control he felt. My husband and I, though, thought it was cool and actually funny. We watched the team move Nate's head from side to side. They made his feet come up off the bed and also wiggled his toes. They moved his hands and other body parts. It was amazing to see how greatly God has blessed human minds such as scientists and doctors.

Cortical mapping helps the neurologists map the surgery. It helps them find out what parts of the brain will affect Nate's other body functions. After cortical stimulation, Nate was ready for the surgery. I could not wait. Focal cortical resection, in which most of the seizure-causing part of Nate's brain was removed, was completed. The surgeons did not remove the entire part of his brain that was affected because that portion touched the portion that controlled mobility on his left side.

After this surgery, Nate was discharged in the worst physical shape that he had ever been in. Having a part of his brain cut out was tough. My husband and I did not think Nathanael would walk again or ever be the same, although the surgeon had reassured us that he would eventually recover. Dr. Wetjen had told us that it would take Nathanael at least a year to recover from this surgery. This was hard for me to digest, especially after my son had had many brain surgeries and had gone back to normal within less than two weeks each time. This time, Nathanael came home in a wheelchair after a full month of staying in the hospital. He could not move his arms and could hardly turn his head. He was shaking almost all the time. What helped was the reassurances I had gotten from his surgeon and his neurologist, which encouraged me to stay hopeful in spite of how Nate looked.

I was off work for two full months to care for Nathanael: the first month in the hospital and the second month at home. (I very rarely accumulated any sick time at work because I was out a lot for my son's hospital visits and doctor's appointments, or at home caring for him.) During these two months, my coworkers at Hospice of the Twin Cities, where I served as a chaplain, blessed me unexpectedly—and in a way I will never forget. They donated their own sick time to me so that I had income for the time when I was out of work. This is one of the ways God has showed His faithfulness for Nathanael's sake. I had not told my coworkers that I had no sick time or that I didn't know how my family was going to get through that time. Although I was remarried, my husband and I had not moved in together during our first year of marriage because we still had many things to sought out concerning trying to merge two family into one. I was totally amazed by God's grace and my coworkers' generosity.

Nate's recovery was extremely slow. He eventually got out of the wheelchair and started walking. However, he could not move his left hand. The neurologist ordered a cast for his right hand, forced him to use his left hand. The cast was kept on for a full month. That was hard for Nate, but the cast was very helpful.

By the time the cast was removed, Nate had regained the use of his left hand. A few months after the surgery, he started going for physical therapy and occupational therapy. I had returned to work. This was another strenuous time in my family's life. After work, I had to take my son for therapy, which started off being almost every day and which tapered off over the months. It was a long tough recovery for Nate and I can't imagine how it felt for him emotionally and physically. He sometimes expressed his frustration with the suffering in his life and wondered why God did not heal him in spite of all the prayers. Although it was exhausting for me, thinking of what it was like for Nate made me chose not to give up.

Nathanael functioned more slowly than he had before the surgery. It took him almost two years to get back to his normal self. Meanwhile, the seizures returned, but they were not as bad as before. These seizures were mild, and very short in length. Nate's neurologist Dr. Nickels had already determined that Ketogenic diet might help Nate if the surgery did not totally take care of the seizures. The team had thought it best to avoid interfering with his left side mobility and instead follow up with other options if need be.

The fact is that Nate's surgery was well worth it, because it changed his life for the better. The seizures that came back were so mild and almost unnoticeable. The next brain surgery he had was shunt related a year and half after the big surgery that was also performed by Dr Wetjen. It is after this surgeries that we have not had ER visit for almost 2 years which while it was a norm prior to this. Prior to the last two years, Nate's insurance was maxed within the first two months of the each calendar year.

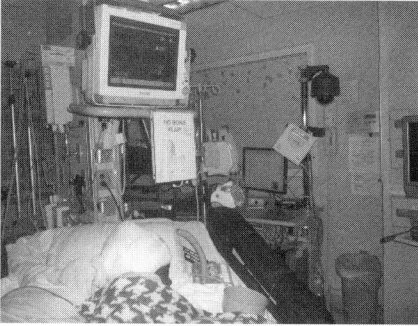
A really scary time

Sally comforts her big brother

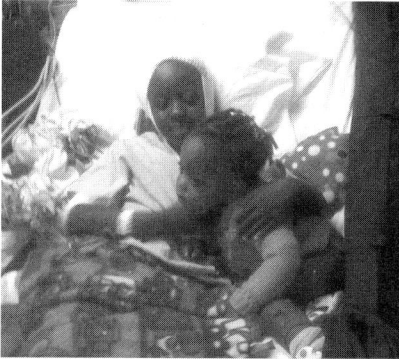
Nate, the big brother
to his sister, Sally

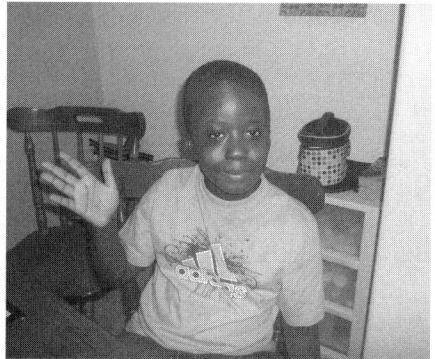
Nate was very weak after the surgery.
He couldn't lift his left arm at all.

Nate gets the cast, which forces
him to use his left hand.

The Ketogenic Diet

The Ketogenic diet, comprised almost entirely of fats and protein, is a diet devised to treat severe seizure disorders that do not respond to conventional medication. It has been around since the 1920s and still proves to work. Studies show that children who follow it for a few years see their seizures reduced by at least 90 percent. Many others become seizure-free, and some are able to stop taking medication. Since the Ketogenic diet is extremely difficult to follow, doctors recommend it only for children who do not respond well to medication.

Even the number of calories in soap, toothpaste, and anything used on the skin are calculated when one is on the Ketogenic diet. A simple sneak of a mint or candy to a Ketogenic patient can cause a severe seizure.

This diet is usually started in the hospital so that the patient can be monitored for a few days to make sure there are no problems. By eliminating carbohydrates from the diet, the body is forced to burn fat for energy, a process called ketosis. This ketosis is the same process that kicks in when someone is fasting or starving. Traditional fasting has been a treatment for seizures for centuries.

When a person is on a Ketogenic diet, everything he or she eats must be precisely weighed, which becomes tiresome to do after two years. The patient's diet is controlled by a neurologist and managed by a dietician. The dieticians help parents and patients adapt to the strict rules of the diet by helping make menus for the patient. As I got used to the diet, the dieticians helped me plan menus with foods that Nate enjoyed more.

No one understands why a Ketogenic diet works, but the fact is that it has been proven to work. Also, it is safe when fully followed. It almost goes without saying that it is challenging for some parents to keep their children on this diet. Many children may accept food from others at school or at parties. Some children may sneak food at home that they shouldn't eat while on this diet. Some older children will eat what they like to eat anyway, so it is hard to keep them on this high-fat, no-carbohydrates diet. This diet therefore works best for younger children who have had limited exposure to foods. In short, the Ketogenic diet is hard work. A parent agreeing to put his or her child on this diet must be prepared for it heart and soul. But it is well worth it.

The Miracle of the Diet

The focal cortical resection surgery did not completely get rid of Nathanael's seizures because the part of his brain that caused the seizures was left intact, as the team did not want to remove it and thereby compromise Nate's left side mobility. Being that Nathanael struggles with medications, his neurologist Dr. Nickels introduced me to the idea of a Ketogenic diet. I had never heard of it before, so she educated me on it and told me how it works. At first, it sounded very scary as I listened to the diet's guidelines, which a patient was expected to follow completely. After telling me about the diet, Dr. Nickels gave me time to think about it. I went home and prayerfully thought about it. I also talked to Nate more about it helping him understand what it all means for him and what his responsibility would be. I talk to him about things that concern him, because I believe in helping him take responsibility for his life. To my surprise, Nathanael was very agreeable to the idea of going on the diet. He hated having seizures and was so tired of them that he was willing to do anything that might stop them from happening. I explained to Nathanael how difficult it would be to follow the diet. He promised me that he would comply fully. Nathanael is an extremely strong-willed child and extremely disciplined. Once he makes up his mind about something, he follows through with it. Although he was a mere ten years old, I trusted his word regarding his decision to follow the diet. I informed his neurologist that we were ready to start the diet. An appointment was scheduled right away. Nathanael was hospitalized for close to a week at the Mayo Clinic to start the diet. During that time, staff members trained us, showing us how to work with the diet. Nate handled this hospitalization well. He was then discharged to me, and the fun began.

The first thing we had to do when we got home was to go grocery shopping. We had all the instructions, the menus, and a list of specific foods to buy. For the time when Nathanael was on the Ketogenic diet, he could only use baby soap for bathing. He could only use Vaseline petroleum jelly on his skin, natural Burt's Bees beeswax lip balm on his lips, and Arm & Hammer toothpaste made of baking soda and peroxide for brushing his teeth. He could not use anything else on his skin.

Shopping for his food was fun. We bought all the ingredients and, of course, a gram scale for weighing his food. It was the hardest shopping I had ever done. After the first few times of carrying our list of instructions to the store, we got familiar with what to buy, so shopping became easier. My husband, who is extremely patient and who loves children, helped out, going out of his way to find foods that fit Nate's diet. All the while, I checked in with Nathanael about his new diet, telling him that it was going to be difficult. He drank some olive oil with every meal, drank heavy whipping cream, ate a little bit of meat or an egg, and then enjoyed some fruit, about half a grape. Sound fun?

Nate's first month on the Ketogenic diet went fine. In fact, he seemed to be doing great on it. He was still having mild seizures, spaced weeks or months apart. After his first month of being on the diet, however, came a new problem. Nathanael started vomiting almost every day during or after dinner. From talking to his medical team, I learned that Nathanael was struggling with constipation. This was a scary time for me, as I wondered if Nate's constipation would lead to even worse complications. He was put on MiraLax, which did not quite take care of the problem.

My husband and I realized that it was when Nate ate meat more often that he was constipated. When he ate eggs instead of meat, he had less of a problem with constipation. This fact took us several months to figure out. Meanwhile, it was my job to clean up Nate's vomit almost every day during or after dinner, and many times with breakfast as well. About a year later, Nate's vomiting lessened, but the cost of being on the diet was great to Nathanael. His cholesterol level got too high on account of all the eggs he ate. After his dieticians learned of this fact, Nate was limited to eating egg whites most of the time, with a few meats here and there. What kept my family sane during this time was our focus on why Nate was on this diet. Otherwise, it would've been hard for us to watch him struggle.

Nathanael completely understood why he was on the diet and took full responsibility for it. He didn't think of cheating, no matter what the circumstance. Kids at school were so sweet and brought him a piece of fruit when they had a birthday party and had brought cupcakes for the other kids. Nathanael always remembered to tell his classmates that he had to take the fruit home so that his mom could weigh it for him and let him know how much he should eat with his meal. My husband and I never had to watch over his diet at home, and the school didn't have to watch over his diet at all. He simply kept to his diet of his own accord. When I gave him something new to eat, he always asked, "Are you sure I can eat this, Mom?" He made the fact that he was on this diet easy on everyone else. Nathanael is a super trouper. He makes his family proud.

The Ketogenic diet is truly miraculous. After a year of being on it, Nate saw his seizures completely vanish. Things got so good that I started to heal from the trauma of expecting his seizures. When I went to work, I could actually leave my phone on a table in my office when I went to the bathroom and not have a panic attack when I remembered I did not have my phone with me. That's how good things got. I was not getting as many phone calls from school to pick up Nathanael. I am still in awe of God and of the medical team at the Mayo Clinic in Rochester.

Nathanael today is living a stable life and serving as a junior board member of City's Heart Cry Ministries, which is geared toward building homes for orphaned and abandoned children in Kenya. He is very passionate about helping every person who lives with pain, especially children.

Nate's Ketogenic meal: olive oil, heavy whipping cream, beef, carrots, and water (while tapering off)

Egg white, orange, heavy whipping cream, and water while tapering off of the Ketogenic diet

The place of Nathanael's miracle! God bless the Mayo Clinic.

Helping Nate Cope with the Diet

As a family, we did not change our diet on account of Nathanael's diet. Many people asked if it was hard for us to change our diet and were surprised when I replied that we did not change our diet. Only Nathanael changed his diet. As a mom, I choose to raise my children for real life. I started by helping Nathanael embrace the Ketogenic diet as his own choice, even if he was only ten years old at the time. I believe in teaching children the reasons why things are a certain way instead of being in control of their every move. In my experience, when I take time to help them understand why, I don't get much fight from them. I can't make everyone in the world change their way of life to meet my needs or my children's needs. I have to help my children cope well in the world they live in. I believe that coping starts at home.

It was hard at first to see Nate eat the foods he was eating while we continued to eat as normal. But in my opinion, it was the right thing to do. If Nathanael could cope with his family's continuing to live a normal life, then he sure could cope with other people's living their lives as he lived his life. My husband and I talked about Nate's feelings and helped him process his own view of life. Once we got past the initial struggle as a family, we accepted Nate's special diet as a part of our normal family life. Nathanael did not want to have seizures. It did not matter to him what he ate as long as he did not have seizures. There were days when he missed eating something we were eating, or that other kids were eating at school. We encouraged him to express his feelings, and we also revisited our choices and the reasons for our choices. I found many articles about people struggling with different medical conditions or sicknesses. We watched videos of people with limitations who had turned their limitation around to help others. This always helped Nathanael feel better. He was determined to make it. Overall, he handled the whole period with a lot of grace and courage, never cheating on his diet. He has come to a place in his young life where he realizes that his medical complication cannot keep him from fulfilling his God-given purpose in life. He has had moments of sadness along the way, but he never sits in self-pity. There were many times when he asked my husband, Nate's stepdad whom he chooses to call "Dad," to help him make chocolate cake for his sister, Sally, and me. Chocolate cake is Nathanael's favorite dessert. My husband and Nate would buy the ingredients and then bake the cake for us. Nathanael enjoyed watching us eat the cake he had made although he could not eat it. He celebrated other people's enjoyment and never let his suffering get in the way of celebrating others' blessings. He many times asked me to buy cupcakes to take to his friends at school for special events and on his birthday even though he could not eat them. He had birthday parties to which his friends were invited. The other children ate whatever they wanted to eat at these parties, and Nathanael enjoyed watching them do so. He is simply an amazing child with an extremely big heart.

Nathanael has had a year and half with no hospitalizations, which is amazing when considering how many times he had been hospitalized previously. He has succeeded with the Ketogenic diet and with everything else he has been through. It has been amazing to watch God work in my son's life through doctors and the many other people involved. Nathanael is truly a miracle.

The Miracle in Nathanael's Function

It is true that God is not limited to human understanding. It is wonderful to see Nathanael living his life like nothing bad had ever happened to him. God operates through this child's physically limited brain in the most amazing way. Looking at his brain images today is the same experience for me as the first time I saw the ultrasound images of him in my womb. Today Nate is doing everything a twelve- to thirteen-year-old is expected to be doing. He goes to school, does chores at home, makes his own bed neatly every morning, keeps his room tidy without being reminded, learns to cook, reads with his younger sister, and so forth. He is respectful, loving, thoughtful, and caring. I have unexpectedly received many thank-you letters from him for one reason or another, or just for being his mom. He truly is a gift.

Nate's Spiritual Development

Nathanael is a very deep child spiritually. As a mom, I am a believer in God's love and power through Jesus Christ, which I intentionally demonstrate to my children from the moment they are born. Even though I haven't been a perfect human being and I have many shortcomings, I press on, living in the light of God's amazing grace. I do not believe solely in teaching my children faith; I believe in living by faith. I believe I am here because God wants me here for a reason. I have been through a lot of painful times in my adult life, but I have never blamed God for it or walked away from Him. I have learned to run to Him for everything, as I have often seen His faithfulness displayed. It is from this mind-set that I raise my children. In our family, we do not take anything for granted. I believe that if my children have God in their lives, they have everything they need to get through life. As a single mother, I prayed with Nathanael. He started to memorize Scripture at a very young age. We watched Bible shows together many times instead of kids' shows.

At the age of four years and eight months, Nathanael gave me the surprise of my life. One night he, of his own accord, told me that he wanted Jesus to come into his heart. I had never preached to him about this or even tried to explain to him this concept. All I did was pray with him every night and every morning. I read to him from the Bible every night before he went to bed. I went to church with him every Sunday, because I believe in being a part of a group of God's people and worshiping with them. There is something beautiful about the fact that God's people gather regularly to worship and praise Him together. I was raised in a family who regularly attended church. It worked for me, so I am doing the same for my children.

While I hadn't expected Nate to understand what it meant to call Jesus into his heart at that age, I did not doubt him either. I have observed some unique things about Nathanael while raising him. He has always been spiritually in tune and has always had faith in God. From a very early age, he asked to pray about many things. He still does so today. On that night when he told me that he wished to ask Jesus into his heart, I led him in prayer. He repeated after me and asked Jesus to come into his heart and lead his life. When we were done praying, he stated, "Again, Mom. I wanna do it again!" We went through it again. I could see the excitement in this little child's eyes. There was such a spiritual connection. I knew his heart understood what he was doing. When we were done praying, he wrapped his little arms around my neck and gave me a big hug, stating, "I love you, Mom." He then lay down peacefully in his bed. I sat and read to him as I watched him fall asleep. It was a joyous, special night for me before the Lord. I was pleased that my young son was owning his faith, which is what he would need to get him through life.

Nathanael, almost thirteen years old today, has only grown deeper in his faith. My husband and I are amazed about how connected he is to the things of God. Many mornings when I check to make sure he is awake and getting ready for school, I find him sitting at the edge of his bed reading the Bible or a devotional before he gets dressed. This is something he started doing on his own. Our role as parents is to train up a child in the way he should go and to trust God to work in our children and to sustain them.

Nurturing Nate's Emotional Development

Having a medical condition that sets you apart is never easy, especially for a child. Children want to be children and to be around other children. Children want to be free to play, to love, and to be loved. Children want to feel accepted, especially by those who are part of their daily lives. It is hard to limit a child from being a child, yet sometimes it is necessary.

Because of Nathanael's medical condition, he has had many limitations placed upon him. His head always must be protected, for example. There are many things he will never be able to do, such as climb mountains, dive, and play football. He can't play in a group of kids who are playing rough, which boys like to do. I have worked to provide him as normal a life as is possible, but it has not always been easy for me. He can play with the children at school, but an adult has to watch him intently when he does so. At home, we make sure he has friends around. We have to watch him intently too. But it has made a big difference to teach Nate responsibility for himself.

As he was able to comprehend what I was saying, I talked to Nathanael about his condition and what he must do to protect himself. Even though he is provided with intentional care at home and at school, he is very good at taking care of himself most of the time. He is also a true kid and experiences times when he does not want to miss out on the fun, such as when other kids are playing. Many of his teachers have been very kind to him. My goal is to help Nathanael be confident. I communicate this to those involved in his life outside of home. In his younger years, especially before his battle with the seizures, he went to a charter school. The teachers there treated him very well. They were very compassionate and supportive. He never felt treated differently from the other kids or left out, even though the teachers watched over him. When Nate had seizures, his teachers kept him safe. They also helped him feel good about himself. I am thankful for the staff of LoveWorks Academy.

My spending a lot of time with Nathanael was the most helpful thing for his emotional development. When I was a single mother, I spent time building him up, listening to him, and showing him that he was my biggest priority. I encouraged him to express his feelings. listened to him and helped him see suffering as a normal part of life. We talked of ways to cope with suffering. We talked about other people who have fought through suffering and have gotten through it. We talked about how normal it is to have feelings of sadness and discouragement sometimes. We talked and talked and talked about the positive things of life and of possibilities. We came up with confessions, which we made together every day. Here is an example: "I am special. I am handsome. I am important. God made me for a purpose. I can do what God says I can do. God loves me. God cares about me. I am loved and accepted. I love myself. I accept myself. I am a helper. I am healed and free."

These things, among other things that we developed depending on our need, were confessed out loud every day from the time when Nate started speaking. He always loved, and still loves, doing these confessions. I believe they play a big part in how he views himself and the world around him.

Family and friends are an important part of Nathanael's life. The more positive relationships a person has, the better it is for his or her emotional stability. My family of origin live in Kenya. I have intentionally made sacrifices to keep my children connected to their relatives in Kenya. When we go to Kenya, we spend almost the entire time with family. This is because I love my family there and want my son to connect with them. He has grown up knowing his grandparents, aunts, uncles, and cousins very well in spite of the distance. He also has maintained some of his friendships with people who have been close to him since he was a baby.

125

Nate's having many people who have shown a continuous personal interest in him has helped him feel good about himself.

Because I trained Nate to accept personal responsibility early in his life, it has stuck with him. I helped him learn to do things for himself and eventually taught him how to help around the house. This made him very proud of himself. In spite of Nate's medical struggle, I choose not to spoil him. I wanted to raise him for his future life. I believe that such training begins the moment a child is born. Starting with speaking faith to a baby and praying audibly once a baby is born onward, how you speak and act around the house when you least think a child is learning etc, is all part of training a child. Nathanael, now age twelve, keeps his bedroom clean and neat. He washes dirty dishes and then puts them away. He puts away his own laundry after it's clean— neatly and in the right places. He vacuums the house when asked to and is attempting to learn how to cook. Nathanael reads a lot of books to his sister, Sally, who, at the age of four, was able to read because of how much time she spends reading together. All of these things make Nate very proud of himself.

My Steve and I intentionally provide a stable home for our children. We do not call the children names or yell at them. I will not stand for any person calling my children names or putting them down and although it is not the easy thing to do, I have stood tall against this kind of behavior when I have had to. I believe that I am an advocate for my children. For the most part, other people will treat your children the way you show them to. I intentionally work to provide a solid environment for my kids. I talk to them about different environments and show them how they can deal with negative environments when there are no parents around. I help them to set good boundaries for themselves and to be okay with choosing how they want to live their lives instead of trying to fit in. I encourage them always to be themselves and not to copy other kids. I am intentional about thinking of the effects of what surrounds my children. I spend a lot of time with them and talk a lot with them.

From the moment I decided to hold out faith for Nathanael before he was born, I decided I was going to do what faith called me to do. That is action! When Nathanael was born, I started raising him as a normal child even though I was told he was not expected to function. When I received paperwork to apply for disability money after he was born, I ripped the papers to pieces, because I did not want to do anything that went against what I believed was best for my child. I refused to apply for that money, instead choosing to work. I nurtured Nathanael with love and also with discipline as he continued to grow. I did not let him get away with throwing tantrums just because he had a medical condition. I disciplined him. What I kept in mind was that Nathanael would eventually be with other people who would not feel for him as much as I do. I did not want him to behave in such a way that would make people despise being around him. I wanted him to behave in such a way that people would love him and not grow tired of him. Nathanael is very gracious and receives a lot of grace back from people in his life. He does not cause trouble, which makes relating to people easy. It also helps his emotional development.

Since Nate can't play most sports, my Steve and I encourage him to focus on doing things that are safe for him. He understands how to take care of himself physically, and he does a great job of it for his age. When he started his battle with seizures, he needed coaching on how to take care of himself. Many times he would start running toward me when he experienced an aura and realized he was about to have a seizure. I had to coach him for a while before he learned simply to sit down and call out for help, which most times he learned to do. When he started talking about how embarrassed he was about having seizures, I talked with him about people who had medical conditions through no fault of their own. Nate had started trying to hide in a bathroom when he had a seizure, but after I talked with him about that, he stopped hiding. All in all, talking about situations instead of avoiding them really helped. Nathanael is emotionally very stable and is a very happy child with a positive outlook on life. He is a joy to be around.

Ever since my Steve has been in Nathanael's life, he has been a godsend. He has been a rock, helping Nathanael satisfy the craving for an adult male in his life. Nathanael has always wanted to be a man, desiring to be around any male who would make time for him. When he was four, a very cute age, he talked of wanting to grow up so that he could marry his mom. I reminded him that he could not ever marry his mom. I said that God would bring the right woman into his life when the time came for him to wed. It didn't make sense to him right away, but I kept giving him the same answer. I wanted to make it clear that he will always be my child. I also told him that God would eventually send a man to be my husband. Eventually, Nate started asking me when I was going to get married so that he could have a dad in his life. I told him that we needed to pray about that. Many times, he remembered to pray during our prayer time together, asking God to send him a dad. Steve came as the answer to that prayer. Steve, a family man, is very involved as a parent. He is conscientious about Nathanael's safety and development. I can see their feelings of fulfillment, especially when they go off together to do men stuff like riding bikes along a trail, working on a home project together, and doing Nate's homework together. God answers prayers.

Raising My Son to Be a Victor

As Nathanael continued to grow, he became self-conscious when other children asked him about the scars on his head. He asked if he could start wearing a hat to cover his head. I did not think it was a good idea. What about the people without a leg or an arm? What about the person whose eye has been removed? I did not want my son to feel ashamed of the scars, so prayerfully we starting working on this matter together. I found articles to share with Nate about people who had physical things they could not hide and how they overcame their limitations and embarrassment. Nate and I talked about Jesus and how He was beat up publicly. We talked about the scars on His body. I encouraged Nate to think of how powerful it could be if he inspired people through his own story. If he covered the scars on his head, no one would ask about them. Leaving them uncovered gave him an opportunity to tell others what God has done for him. I encouraged him to express his feelings, which we then processed together.

Nathanael does wear hats, but not for the reason he originally wanted to wear them. He likes hats and will wear them on occasion, but he has become very comfortable with his scars. He actually stops to respond positively when people ask about his scars, which happens often. He is growing into wanting to share his testimony so as to give God glory for how far He has brought him. More and more, Steve and I see evidence that Nate is proud of himself, especially when he gets an opportunity to testify about God.

At home, Steve and I continue to teach Nate age-appropriate life skills. He continues to be positive and does not grumble when he is asked to put away dishes, to load the dishwasher, or to do any other chore. A great big brother, he helps his sister out as well. She adores him. My husband has taught Nate how to ride a bike and how to swim. They also do male-specific things together. Steve is very deliberate about keeping Nathanael safe while they are hanging out together, which Nathanael loves to do. Steve is a great role model for what a man is supposed to be for his wife and for what a dad should be for his children. Nathanael has made comments like, "I wanna learn to cook so that I can help my wife out when I get married."

Living amid a community of people is important. Steve and I talk to Nate about the law and the importance of respecting the law of the land. We keep strong boundaries at home and train Sally and Nate to exercise simple respect at home. I believe that children should respect their parents, because that is the base for human life. I believe that if a child can learn to respect his parents when he is young, he will most probably respect those in authority when he is grown. I do not want my children to grow up with the mentality that they can do whatever they want to do in life. Life is full of rules and boundaries. I want my children to learn to keep to their own space while they are young so that they don't get lost when they step out into the rough world.

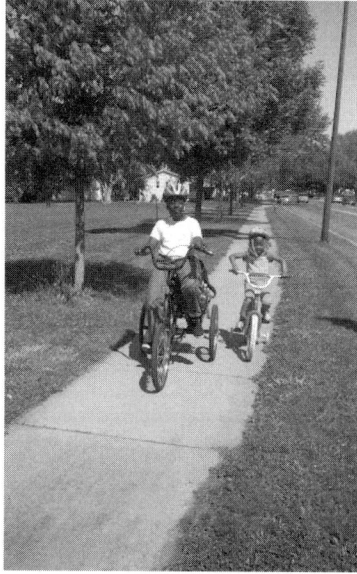
Nate and Sally riding their bikes

Nate and Sally ready for breakfast

I thank God for my children.

Part Four

As a Caregiver

Mountains and Valleys

Life is a mystery that we cannot understand.
We are born into a world over which we have no control.
When the sun shines, she shines as she wishes.
Right at noonday, the rain pours as it wishes.
I wonder time and time again. My wonder never ceases.
In the midst of my wondering, our wonderful God reigns.

Mountains fall ahead; valleys, beneath our feet.
We weaken and we faint as we climb up the mountains.
We stumble and we slide going down the valleys.
We choose no mountains and no valleys.
We hurt in the mountains and hurt down in the valleys.
In the midst of our hurting, our God hurts for us.

Mountains and valleys do not last forever.
A short while they may last, leaving us stronger.
Pain is not forever; neither is sorrow.
When we are at our weakest, Jehovah is almighty.
We don't understand, but our God understands.
Our hope and our strength rests in His might.

Mountains are high, but God is higher.
Valleys go deep, but God goes deeper.
Our tears get hot, but our Lord's tears were mixed with blood.
In the midst of our hurting, our Lord hurts more.
We have no control; He has full control.
Victory smiles at us as we hope in Him.

—Ann Makena

Ann B. Makena

Care giving

A caregiver is simply a person who regularly takes care of someone who is in a more vulnerable position. A caregiver can be a family member or someone else, paid or not paid. A caregiver may provide care for a child, a sick person (chronically ill or otherwise), an elderly person, or a disabled person. Care giving is basically about taking care of a person who isn't able to take care of himself or herself. A caregiver provides a safe, caring environment for the person for whom he or she cares. While the term *caregiver* describes other people, such as doctors, nurses, and the like, my focus on is on the type of caregiver who cares for a loved one.

Being a caregiver comes with its own challenges, but it also brings satisfaction. Working as a full-time hospice chaplain for many years gave me the opportunity to develop a view of caregivers. I worked with people who were facing death or chronic illness as well as with their families and loved ones. I had the honor of being a part of many people's journeys at a critical time of their lives. I had the honor of processing with many people the important things of their lives, to help them come to a place of peace before they died. I sat with many people as they took their last breaths. I prayed with many of them right before they died. I had the honor of conducting numerous bedside services for families while they said their good-byes to their loved one before and after he or she died. I had the honor and privilege of officiating numerous funerals, memorial services, and burials, all for wonderful people for whom I had provided care before they died. Being a hospice chaplain was one of the most humbling experiences of my entire life. It helped me to put many things into the right perspective at a young age. I came to terms with how real death is for everyone. This made me more intentional about evaluating my own life regularly and focusing on things that were most important, like my relationship with God and with the people in my life. I realized, more than any theory could teach me, that every day of my life is a gift to be cherished and to be lived with passion.

What impacted my life as a caregiver was my support of other caregivers in the situations in which I worked. I watched the pain in the eyes of caregivers as they watched their loved one fade away in their presence. I was involved in situations where caregivers had to make life-or-death decisions for their loved ones, having to deal with the feelings that go along with the outcomes of such decisions. I watched many patients yell at their caregivers about things the latter could not change. I watched caregivers spend sleepless nights beside the bed of their loved one and then walk around half asleep during the day. I listened to many stories of things that caregivers went through in providing care for their loved ones, including traumatic experiences they had during their loved one's sickness and horrible experiences at a hospital. I witnessed caregivers' worry for their loved ones and their feelings of desperation when they felt they couldn't improve the situation. I witnessed their feelings of being alone and misunderstood, their experiences with not being heard in many situations, and so forth. I came to a realization that caregivers carry a lot of suffering of their own while the person they provide care for suffers.

The situations that I dealt with at work became such a source of comfort for me in my own life as a caregiver. I am sure the families I worked with would have been surprised if they had known what I had been dealing with on some of the days I provided them with support. There were many times when my son was in the hospital when I went to support some of my patients and their families. There were days when I was worried about my son's life, but I still sat with a dying patient at work or conducted a bedside service or a funeral. But that is life. Unfortunately life does not stop for anyone. No matter what you are going through, life continues.

I found comfort in supporting other people in their suffering. I realized that I was not the only person suffering and that many people's situations were worse than mine. I loved my job because it brought fulfillment to my heart. I have a calling to work with people during tough times and through painful situations. I easily feel for people with my heart. Supporting someone when he or she is going through something difficult comes naturally to me. My job was made better for me by the fact that I was struggling through a situation of my own. Supporting others fed my heart. I was always happy to go to work and happy when I came home from work. This is another reason God had brought me to this job: it worked not only for my son's need but also for my need to become the person God intended me to be.

As a caregiver, I went through the same things other caregivers go through. Outside of work, I had to find ways to survive during my own difficult times. I have experienced trauma on account of my son's medical condition, and I have worried a great deal. Physically, I have had to deal with numerous ER visits and with placing calls to make appointments with several doctors. I've dealt with my son's numerous hospitalizations and with answering calls from all the physicians and teams of professionals who treated him. I've also dealt with making calls to pharmacies and then picking up meds. Nate was strongly advised not to skip a dose of anticonvulsants. I remember times when I forgot to call in time to refill his medicine. I had to run around the Twin Cities area, from Walgreens to Walgreens, before Nate's bedtime to find one that had the medicine in stock. That happened after a full day of work, which involved dealing with people during their tough times and driving from one person's home to the next all day long. There were times when I felt like my body was melting in tiredness. The two and half years when Nate was on the Ketogenic diet topped it off. I had to weigh everything that went into Nathanael's mouth for those two years, everything other than water. I spent at least an hour each day preparing his food for that day. It took him a very long time to eat because of what he had to consume for every meal. I also had to clean up a lot of vomit after dinner, particularly during his first year of being on the diet. Nate felt terrible about throwing up uncontrollably which made me stay positive because I wanted him to know, I knew he did not mean to throw up.

I have spent countless sleepless nights and, for an extended period of my life, was a single mother with my family living in another country. I have sometimes cried until I could not cry anymore, although most people I know cannot imagine me crying that much. Many times I did not know what to pray for. I heard stories of people who had seizures at night and who died as a result. That would keep me sleepless for several nights, fearing that the same might happen to my child. I worked for a hospice, which kept death very real in my mind. This made me become intentional about finding ways to cope.

Prayer and assertiveness

An After-Midnight Surgery

It was one of those days when I knew that my son, Nathanael, needed immediate attention. He was about two years of age when this happened. When we left home, he was vomiting a lot and seemed very lethargic. He very sick, and I knew it. When we got to a hospital, he was treated. A CT scan revealed that he needed surgery, which I had expected to be the case. He was admitted.

Once we got to the floor where his room was, he lit up at the sight of the playroom and other kids' attractions. At that moment, a nurse practitioner arrived to check on the status of Nathanael. She found a child who was playing.

It was a Friday afternoon. Even though there was a spot for surgery that afternoon, the nurse practitioner decided that Nathanael could wait until Monday, seeing as he was under observation. Since the time of his arrival the hospital, the staff had ordered him not to eat in case he needed to be ready for surgery. The nurse practitioner gave him the okay to eat. I tried to reason with her, saying how sick Nathanael was, but she did not agree with me. She stated that she regularly dealt with kids who had hydrocephalus and that, as far as she could tell, Nathanael could wait until Monday for surgery. Like has happened to me a few other times with other medical professionals, this nurse practitioner thought that I as a caregiver had poor judgment about Nathanael's condition because he was my own child and refused to consider my input being the person with this child every day. I knew how sick he was that day.

The staff went ahead and fed Nathanael. As soon as he finished eating, he started vomiting nonstop. This was a long period of projectile vomiting, vomit that went all over the room. The nurse called the neurosurgery team, who did not arrive quickly. Their nurse practitioner had told them how well Nathanael was doing, and they took her word for it—although she had seen Nathanael for only few minutes—over the word of the person who was raising him and who was with him every day. Nathanael kept vomiting. The nurses on the floor became upset about it and called the neurosurgical team again. At last Nathanael got so sick that somehow a decision was then made that he would have surgery immediately. The surgeon was called at his home. Nate ended up in an operating room in the middle of the night, precisely at 1:00 a.m.

After that surgery, Nathanael was extremely sick, vomiting right afterward because he had eaten and had not been prepared. It was an emergency surgery. There were a lot of apologies made to me the next morning, but that situation could have been avoided. Not to blame the nurse practitioner, who made an observation upon which she based her decision. But I don't agree with a system that totally disregards a caregiver's opinion, counting it as mere worry without doing further investigation—and that was what happened on that day. Nathanael's appearance and actions happen to be deceptive when it comes to his being sick or in pain. He hides his condition well, especially when he is determined to do something like play or go somewhere. I have gone through similar situations with him, where he makes a fool of me before other people realize how sick he is. When Nathanael looks sick, it is emergent.

Another thing happened after Nate had had surgery and was still in the hospital for observation. The surgeons had ordered neurological checks like they normally do after brain surgery. The night nurse came to do the neuros, as they are referred to in the hospital, while my son was sleeping. (I slept in the hospital every night of my son's hospitalization, and I am thankful to God for that.) On that night, I was just falling asleep when I heard my child sleepily say, "No! *No!*" I jumped out of my sleeping corner in the room and went through the curtain to find a nurse holding my child tightly down on his bed. Her knees were holding his knees down, and one of her hands was tightly holding both his little hands. In the nurse's mouth was the light used for doing neuros. She was forcing Nate's eyes open with one of her hands. Nate was moving his head from right to left in protest, stating, "No! No!"

The nurse did not stop until she heard my voice. I was very angry, as you can imagine. I said, "Stop!"

The nurse let go of Nate, stood, looked at me, and stated, "I have to do it! It's a doctor's order!" I have never been more upset. I demanded she leave the room immediately.

She repeated angrily, "It's a doctor's order!" I did not argue with her, but I did demand again that she leave the room. I pressed the button to call for a nurse. A different nurse entered the room. I asked to see the charge nurse. I was breathing fire.

The nurse who was sent to do the neuros hadn't first spoken to my child to tell him what she was about to do. She did not show any compassion while he moved his head on the bed after having had brain surgery. She was more concerned with fulfilling the doctor's order than she was with caring for Nate.

After I told the charge nurse what had happened, she was apologetic and supportive. Nathanael was not a child who fought the staff. He has had many needles and IVs placed in his body, and he always held still for the insertion process. All the nurse had to do was to explain to him what she was about to do. The charge nurse took care of my son for the remainder of that night, and the nurse who had held Nathanael down didn't take care of him after that. Out of his many hospital stays, that was the only time I had observed a health care provider behave that way toward him. But I have heard similar stories from other people.

As a caregiver, you can't just sit back and watch another person maltreat your child (or other loved one) and do nothing about it. Yet doing something about it may open you up to criticism and gossip. Staff members like the nurse who had held down Nate often will not admit to what they did. They will do what is called "covering their butt." Thankfully, that situation did not get messy for Nate.

Having to deal with the type of situation just described, even though such occasions have been rare, has led me to being more prayerful and assertive. I often pray for God's protection, because situations do arise that I am not expecting. When God is involved, things do seem to work out, even if they start out tough. Prayer also helps me feel lighter as I give my heavy situations to God. Many things happen in my life that are out of my control. It helps me to come to terms with that fact and to give control to someone who can do something about the situation. God works from the inside out, working in ways that we cannot fathom. He speaks to people on my behalf, in ways that I cannot speak to them. I have prayed many times that He would speak on my behalf, especially to doctors. As a result, I did not have to try to get my point across myself. Prayer also keeps my heart at peace during the stormy, rocky times. Being aware of God's presence changes everything. It gives me grace to persevere and courage when I need courage.

As a caregiver, being assertive is critical. Assertiveness does not equal rudeness or disrespect. Being assertive simply means being confident of what you know to be true. It means being bold, firm, and determined about what you need get to across. Many caregivers live with the fear of how they are being perceived, which makes them back down when they should be speaking up for their loved ones. I have been in that situation myself. Over time, I have learned to focus on what is really important, and that is not how others perceive me. What is important is what my child needs at any given time. Being assertive does not turn good willed professionals against me, as I sometimes fear will happen to me as a caregiver. Instead, it actually helps me get the right care, and sooner.

Being a caregiver is tough, as you have to deal with being misunderstood from time to time. You also have to deal with people. Generally speaking, people are complex no matter who they are. I have found a lot of peace in the power of prayer and also in standing up for what I know to be true. Through raising my son, I have come to terms with the fact that not everyone will listen to what I am saying. But I will not stop speaking of what I know to be the needs of my loved ones until someone, somewhere, has heard me.

Life in Constant Trauma

Trauma arises from a deeply distressing or disturbing experience. Because different people handle different events in different ways, what is traumatic to one person may not be so to another. Trauma leaves a person feeling overwhelmed, helpless, in pain, confused, and trapped. A person who experiences trauma may develop a fear of death or feel that someone else has abused his or her power and betrayed his or her trust. *Trauma* is a broad term describing the psychological, physical, and emotional state of a person following an event that was difficult for him or her to handle.

Personally, I have experienced a series of traumatic events over many years. Dealing with trauma became a norm for me, from being abused to undergoing the struggles involved with raising my son, and from having a child out of wedlock and enduring the struggles involved in my relocating from my parents' home to a home in a new country on my own. My son's medical condition has been the heaviest of all because of the length of time and the nature of it. It has been a constant series of run, run, with a lot of emotional, scary situations. I did not know what to expect from day to day. As much as I have faith, I have not found a way to get past my emotions when dealing with my own child's life. Watching

Nate struggle as much as he has is tougher than I can describe. Parents in a situation like mine will be able to understand.

What is it like to go to work and all day feel panic that you might have missed a phone call from school? That was normal for me at one point. What is it like to watch your child having a forty-five-minute seizure when a two-minute seizure feels like hours? What is it like to be having a normal morning and all of a sudden your child has a seizure—and you have no idea when it will happening? What is it like when you are downstairs and your child goes upstairs looking okay, but then within a minute he is calling for help, running toward the stairs, and coming to find you since he is having a seizure. (Nate got aura before the seizure onset and had partial seizures. Once He had auras, he knew a seizure was about to happen and that is when he would start running or calling. Thankfully, each and every time he was in this state, someone was always close enough to hold him and guide him to a sit or ground. Miraculously, as many seizures as he had, Not any single time did he fall or get hurt, praise to God). What is it like to watch your child in the hospital with continuous seizures and vomiting? What is it like to be pregnant and arrive on the scene just to find that your child has quit breathing and there is a troop of medical people surrounding him? What is it like to watch your child lying in bed for two weeks without a piece of bone in his head, knowing how delicate a brain is? What is it like when your child has surgery one day and when your mother, in a different hospital, has surgery the next day—and you are a single mother with no other family around? What is it like to watch and wait for your child to go through twenty surgeries, each time not knowing how it is going to turn out? What is it like to have a near death experience, knowing you have two children who need you? What is it like to be half asleep night after night because you are worried about your child? What is it like to go through these things for a ten-year period? During those years of my life, while I worked for a hospice as a chaplain, many times I felt like I needed a chaplain myself.

Trauma's Effects on Me

One day when I was home with my children, the two of them had just stopped playing and had lain down. I was busy in the kitchen. A bit later, I went to see what they were up to. Sally was about two years old then. I noticed that her head was moving under the covers. Guess what went through my mind? *Seizure! She is having a seizure!* Sally doesn't have seizures, nor does she have any medical condition. Still, I did walk from the kitchen to where she was and, calling her name desperately, grabbed her in my arms. Of course she was in shock. She had a look in her eyes that seemed to ask, *What is going on?* I felt like I had just awakened from a really bad dream once I realized she was okay. I also realized what was happening to me. Poor Sally was left not understanding what had just happened. I reassured her and laid her back under the covers. I can't describe the feelings and thoughts that went through my mind during those few seconds when I saw her head moving. It took me a while to recover from the shock of that moment. There had been nothing wrong that day.

There are many times when I have heard my child make a noise and call out to me. When this happens, my first instinct is always to run as my heart skips a beat. As a result of the many times I have run to catch my son and prevent him from falling during a seizure, my psyche has become trained to cause me to behave that way even when my child is not having a seizure. Sometimes I have flown up the stairs to get to Nate before he has even made it to the first step, thinking that he was having a seizure. I have also experienced the fear that he would die at night during a seizure. Whenever his school called me, which was more times than I can count, my heart skipped a beat as soon I saw the school's number. Many times the school called to inform me of something, to ask a question, or for some other reason. It did not matter why they were calling; during the season when Nate was struggling with seizures, I panicked when I saw the school's number. And if I was at work at the time, my mind started thinking about how fast I could get to my son. Many times the school staff, when they called me, were kind enough to let me know right away that my son was okay before they started to tell me why they had called. I appreciated that.

Needless to say, it has taken the hand of God for me to be here today in one piece. Sometimes I am surprised that I have never walked out of the house wearing my pants on my head. I have never had to take any mood medications, although there have been times when I have felt very stressed out. It has not been easy for me to cope, but the Lord has helped me, giving me the will and the way to get through it.

Committing Our Ways

The sunflower, before the sunrise,
droops down, resting eastward.
At the waking of the rising sun,
she lets her smile unfold, showing her beauty.
She makes me wonder time and again,
Am I aware of God's presence?

The sunflower, at the touch of the rising sun,
spreads her glorious yellow beauty.

As the sun reaches out, keeping her warm,
she thankfully receives it in worship.
She makes me wonder time and again,
Am I aware of God's touch?

The sunflower, at every move of the sun,
Follows courageously with her whole being.
As the sun strolls from east to west,
the sunflower joins the beautiful walk.
She makes me wonder time and again,
Am I following God's leading?

The sunflower, so beautiful and bright,
knows dependence and commitment.
Worship and glory shine as she lives out
A demonstration of joy in following the sun.
She makes me wonder time and again,
Am I committed to following God?

—Ann Makena

Life has been hard for me, as it has been for others. Fearing that I would drown because of the roughness of life on earth led me to find ways of coping. Some of what has worked for me includes, but is not limited to, the things that follow:

A Practice of Spiritual Alertness

Deliberately being aware of God's presence in my life has been the most helpful thing for me. I look for the ways in which God is working in my life each day. There is a secret in Proverbs 3:6

(NKJV): "In all your ways acknowledge Him, And He shall direct your paths." I love to be able to sit back every day and reflect on my day, being thankful to God because I have come to understand that it is not certain that I will return home every night simply because I had planned on doing so. Since I started raising my son, I have never been able to plan ahead with certainty, like I see many people do. I have gotten up to go to work but then have ended up in the hospital more times than I can count. I have had to cancel major plans. I have worked in a setting wherein I met people who were living a normal life one day and who then found themselves in bed the next day, waiting to die within the week. These things have forced me to search my soul and to seek peace along with gratitude for life on a regular basis. The more I acknowledge God for working in my life, the more I see Him and the more my trust in Him grows. I find surrendering to God easier when I have witnessed His faithfulness. Not only does the Bible say that God is faithful, but also I have seen evidence of this in my own life.

Praying is my favorite thing to do. I pause to make prayer a priority, because it gives God the opportunity to work on me in the stillness of the moment. Prayer prepares me for the situations to come and for dealing with what is at hand. I have found that seeking God intentionally brings me more peace than I can fathom in the worst of situations. The peace of God is what I have found to be the most important thing to hold onto, because most times I have no control over the things that happen in my life or around me. Peace is also what helps me know that God is leading me into a situation. When I lack peace about something, it is time for me to stop, and to still my spirit.

Included in my prayers is my worship of God for who He is. When I pray, I like to play worship music and focus my heart on God the person. He is real and likes to relate to His people. One of the things I like to do is to get to know people for who they really are, not just for their work title or social status. When these things are gone, who are we? Similarly, I like to study Scriptures that talk about who God is. I take time to lift up His name. There are many times when I don't feel like doing it. Sometimes I am tired or something is going on that causes me distress, and the last thing I feel like doing is getting into the presence of God to worship Him. I start by forcing myself to do it, as I have found this to work. As I start to tell Him that He is still God in spite of my feelings, I find that His spirit lifts my burdens and makes me aware of His presence. When I spend time worshipping God, a peace follows me around and I see Him work things out before I realize how much I needed His help.

Engaging in Spiritual Warfare

Whether you are aware of this or not, life is full of warfare. Being aware of this and paying attention to your heart helps in very many ways. Since we are spiritual beings living in human bodies, our warfare is spiritual in nature. It only sometimes manifests in the physical realm. In living my life and especially in raising my children, I have gotten better at paying attention. I have also learned many things. The Spirit of God warns us when something is about to happen.

One day, I was praying and I felt in my heart that I should go over to my son's bedroom. It did not make sense to me, but I did it anyway. I started to feel very heavily that I should pray against death. Although my son was struggling, he was coping—and at that moment he was at school. Once I started to pray, I was led to his room. I found myself crying before God for a long time. The following day, during our night prayer at home, my spirit was again filled with emotions. I prayed for my son as I was led to do. I also anointed him with oil, praying for his protection and his life. I took him to an appointment the following day, a Thursday, without knowing that his doctor was going to say that he needed surgery the very next day. Nate had surgery on the following day. That experience made it clear why I had been crying to God for my son's life earlier that week.

Many times, I stop when I feel in my heart a need to stop. I have learned not to wait for understanding before I stop. I miss out on many opportunities when I ignore the small voice inside me. Some years back, I was led to pray for someone who was close and dear to me. She had been struggling. She was supposed to come to my apartment, but she was not feeling well. She called me to let me know she was too tired to drive and was going to sleep at her place. I felt impressed to drive there and to take her back home with me. I didn't go to her place even though my spirit urged me to go. My son was struggling too. I didn't want to take him out of the apartment at night, so I decided to wait to see my friend. I decided to pray for her throughout the week. A day later she died, before I had an opportunity to go and pray with her as I was led to do. She was my age mate. Eventually God gave me grace to move on from that mistake. That episode served as a rude awakening for me.

As spiritual beings, we are connected to each other in ways we cannot understand. We feel things about another person that we have no knowledge of, and about places we have never been to before. Ephesians 6:10 tells us that our war is not against flesh and blood but that it is spiritual. Studying how God worked in biblical times has been helpful to me in my times of spiritual warfare. He is the same yesterday, today, and forever. If He worked then, He still works today. In the same way He brought the wall of Jericho down, He, I believe, will bring down the walls for me. And because

His people won wars with no weapons, I trust Him to win wars for me without my having weapons.

Throughout my son's life, I have used praise and worship as well as warfare music in his bedroom. My children fall asleep to worship music every night. When Nate is in the hospital, I play this music nonstop, as I believe that God then fills the room and brings victory. Sometimes I have played the same song over and over all day long, depending on what is going on. We sing along too. The words we speak make such a difference to what results we receive. I believe when we are singing "Till the Walls Fall" (e.g., "We won't stop praising until the walls come down") or "My God Is a Big God" (e.g., "My God is a big God; He will fight for me") by Martha Munizzi, or other praise and worship music, victory is birthed. This music keeps my spirit encouraged and peaceful in the most trying of times. It helps create an atmosphere that leaves me feeling like nothing serious is happening even when serious things are happening. It also creates an atmosphere of faith, which gives God a table to operate on.

Something that has become evident to me along my journey is that attacks seem to come my way when victory is around the corner or right after I've had a big breakthrough. I remember the time right after my son had the biggest surgery he has ever had. We were very happy, praising God that he had gone through it successfully. All of a sudden, we experienced a slap in the face. This was the second time in Nate's life that he had a very prolonged seizure. After my Nate's big surgery and discharged, we went home, all full of praise, for the success. When we got home that afternoon, after a two and half hour long trip, Nate was very tired and he laid for a nap. He happened to lay too long on the incision which we later believed caused that unexpected long seizure. But at the moment it was happening, we all felt severely discouraged. The reason for this surgery had been to help with the seizures, but he ends up having one of the longest seizures he has ever had. Nate and our were totally confused, felt helpless etc. We called 911 and even rescue medications did not seem to stop the seizure. He was rushed to one of the close hospitals where they monitored him through that night since it was late evening by that time, and transported back the Mayo Clinic the following morning. Imagine what was going through our minds. My son was crying for the entire forty-five minutes of this strange seizure, asking, "Why is this still happening to me after all the prayers, Mom? I thought I was not going to have seizures anymore." It was painful. I felt stabbed through the heart. I was wondering the same thing as my son, but I had to be the strong one. That was such a test. I tried to encouraged my son, because I did not want him to lose faith in God. I told him we had to keep trusting. Deep inside I felt like screaming at God, telling Him how hurt I was for trusting Him, and asking Him what He really had in store for my child and for me!

See, I had used up a great deal of emotion when going through this huge surgery, fully confident that once Nate was through it, he would be in a great place. Then he has this seizure right after the surgery and discharge, one of the worst seizures he has ever had! How confusing is that! I felt like I was crawling on my belly, with pain in my spirit. I am really thankful for my husband, who noticed I was not doing okay. He stepped in, encouraging Nate and praying with him. I listened to Steve tell him, "You are healed, Nate. Don't believe any of what is happening right now. Believe the word of God and His promises"

I wanted to say, "Blah, blah, blah," but I had to behave for my son's sake. At that moment, I was angry. I had no faith left in me. But my God stayed faithful.

When Nathanael got back to the Mayo Clinic, the doctors there did not seem alarmed. They said they had seem this happen after brain surgery even with people who had never had seizures before. Nate was readmitted for observation. They speculated that since Nathanael had laid for nap on the surgical site for several hours on the day of discharge after arriving home, that may have caused irritation to his brain as his brain was still recovering from surgery. Even though fear had sent our family down into the pits for a moment, we were relieved to learn that they see these with other patients after brain surgery and they hoped that's all it was with Nate. Time has proved that it most probably was the irritation because that was the last time we saw that and it has been years since. Going through that was such a test of faith and I can only say I am thankful for God's grace because my attitude did not pass the test during that trial. In spiritual warfare, we need to train ourselves to stand on God word even when faced with giants like this. Thankfully, when we are overtaken by the circumstances like I was, I believe God is gracious and He remains faithful.

Many other times, I have seen things like this happen. Spiritual warfare comes in many ways. Sometimes it comes through people. But we must remember that our warfare is not against flesh and blood. When we let God fight our battles, He keeps us in perfect peace while He puts things in order for us. It has been amazing to see how God works things out for me. No matter how warfare comes, it is important to keep in mind that God's kingdom is under attack. We have to stay ready; otherwise, it is very easy to get thrown off track. Keep in mind Matthew 11:12 (NASB): "From the days of John the Baptist until now the kingdom of heaven suffers violence, and violent men take it by force."

Developing Resilience

"God is our refuge and strength, A very present help in trouble. Therefore we will not fear, Even though the earth be removed, And though the mountains be carried into the midst of the sea; Though its waters roar and be troubled, Though the mountains shake with its swelling" (Psalm 46:1–3 NKJV).

Resilience is the ability to face difficult life situations, for example, trauma, sickness, divorce, and to bounce back without being affected so negatively that you can't continue living effectively. It is the ability to bear, or to recover successfully from, difficult conditions. Some people have more resilience than others, but the good news is that resilience can be developed by any person who is willing to work at it. I believe that resilience begins with the realization that life is not easy but that all things are possible. Secondly, I believe that God is more powerful than anything life or death may bring my way. Giving Him control brings me peace in difficult situations.

When my siblings and I were growing up, our parents often talked to us about life in general and how difficult it can be. They encouraged us never to give up in life and to endure when challenges come our way. This did not make much sense to me until I had a life of my own. Life will always present challenges. On top of that, people are often difficult to deal with, no matter how good their intentions are.

Within a short time of moving to America, I started applying some of the principles my parents had taught me. I had to fight hard to survive the difficulties of moving to a foreign country on my own. I have faced many other life situations since then, and I kept reminding myself that I must not give up. Instead of focusing on the mountains ahead of me, I learned to focus on the Creator of the heaven and the earth and on His ability to move any mountain that stands in my way.

I also learned to listen to other people's stories instead of jumping to conclusions after I saw what was happening in their lives. Knowing the difficulties others are facing keeps me reminded that I am not the only person who is suffering, especially when I feel very weak. Many people have been divorced like I was. Many others have experience with being sick or being betrayed by someone they trusted. Many others have endured worse situations than I have endured, and many of those people have made it through. I listen to and read about what others are doing to overcome. From this, I learn tactics that I can apply to my own situation. I also pray for others and cry for others, which helps me take my focus off my life when things are difficult.

The Bible is the greatest source of my courage during tough times. I search it to find words of encouragement for each situation I face. One of the Scriptures that speaks to my heart in regard to enduring difficult times is Psalm 91.

Having an Inner Awareness Is Helpful

This is one of the most precious of the things that my clinical pastoral education taught me to develop in life. Self-awareness is having a conscious concept of who you are on the inside. It includes coming to terms with your personality, strengths, weaknesses, beliefs, motivation, thoughts, and emotions/feelings. Practicing self-awareness allows you to see where your thoughts and emotions are taking you, which helps you control your behavior, which in turn helps shape your character. Self-awareness also helps you make the changes in your life that you want to make. Being aware in the moment of what you are feeling or thinking helps you control your behavior instead of leading you to act without thinking. Being self-aware makes it easier for you to understand how others perceive you. It helps you relate better and to be received better by others. It is one of the attributes of emotional intelligence that helps you succeed in controlling your emotions. The more you develop self-awareness, the more you have the ability to accept yourself as an individual who is separate from your environment and from others around you. It helps you develop your own worth as a person, refining what you hope for in life.

Going through the process of learning how self-awareness works not only helped me in my journey as a chaplain; it also helped me greatly in my personal life, especially during my journey of being a caregiver. I have learned to be okay with my emotions and my thought process. I have found that in being aware of what is cooking inside me I pay attention how what I feel affect my environment and my responses. I have also learned to express to others what I am feeling and what I need from them. Being a mother and a wife in tough times is now easier for me. I am okay with just being. When I feel like God has deserted me, I accept that this is how I am feeling. I might even talk to someone about how I am feeling or what I am thinking. Many undesirable emotions and thoughts come with being a caregiver. This is normal. I have had to give myself permission to be real.

For example, on the day after a night when I did not get much sleep and I feel crabby as a result, I speak this fact to my husband and children. My mood then lightens, because they make fun of me and of how I am feeling. I find myself laughing with them. When I need space because I am sad or upset about something, I stop and mention what I need. This helps me receive support and keeps me from reaching a point of being unable to control my emotions. Most people are very understanding and are willing to help a caregiver feel better if they know what the caregiver needs.

Taking time to understand myself has helped me to come to terms with what I want in life. It also has helped me choose the people I spend time with. As a caregiver, I realize that it is critical to take care of myself. My circumstances leave me with less to live on than people whose lives are stable have. Some people have told me that I need to have more faith for my child instead of taking him for surgeries. These people meant well and wanted to be supportive. They even hurt for me when I was suffering. All they wanted was to see things get better for me. But some of the things they said to me were not helpful.

I have learned not to talk much about my struggles, because there are not very many listeners. Most people want to tell me what I should do to solve the problems of my life. What I have found to be most helpful are people who will just be with me. Being aware of how people make me feel has been helpful to me as a caregiver.

Self-Educating

"My people are destroyed for lack of knowledge; because you have rejected knowledge, I reject you from being a priest to me. And since you have forgotten the law of your God, I also will forget your children" (Hosea 4:6 ESV).

As the saying goes, knowledge is power. In my life as a caregiver, I have found this simple truth to be very helpful. The more you know about anything, the better it is for you. I am very grateful to have come from a family that emphasized education. I grew up seeing the difference education makes, especially in Africa where there is no welfare system to help people. As an adult, I have found myself wanting to study and understand everything that affects me. In raising my children, I don't settle for what life brings. I like to study everything I can find in regard to what affects them. With Nathanael having medical complications, I read everything I could find in regard to hydrocephalus. My research paper for my psychology major was on the effects of hydrocephalus in children. I wanted to understand as much as I could on the condition so that I knew how best I could help my son. Later on, when Nate started struggling with seizures, I started my study on seizures. I still read on these subjects and about many other conditions of the brain. I like to understand what treatment Nate is being given and why. I like knowing about the possible side effects of the medications he is given and what other options are available. I found out about the surgery to correct his seizures by myself, with God's help. That surgery ended up making a significant change in my child's life.

Many good doctors give caregivers and patients a chance to express what they are looking for, but when a patient or caregiver doesn't know what he or she wants or what the diagnosis means, doctors are forced to make decisions based on their judgment of the person they're trying to help. I like to compare what I have found out on my own with what I observe so that when I talk with the doctors about my child, I am not coming from a place of cluelessness. From the beginning, I realized that my child was very complex and could not be classified. I don't know many people who have had the number of brain surgeries Nate has had. What helped me develop assertiveness in being his advocate and caregiver was studying and acquiring as much knowledge about what affects him as I could. Having this knowledge has also helped me in nurturing Nate, helping him become the man he will become. It is important to do everything we can to understand things that affect our children as well as our lives. When I have understanding,

I can develop boundaries that help shape the future. It also leaves me feeling peaceful knowing that I did everything I possibly could do in the circumstance.

I have also come to realize that nothing I learn goes to waste. The accounting that I hated when I was in school has been helpful to me. It equipped me for dealing with the financial aspects of starting a new organization from scratch. While I was going to school and later working in a nursing facility as a home health aide, I learned a lot about the medical profession, which has made my life much easier, especially when dealing with my son's medical condition and his medications. It was then that I learned how helpful it is to put medications in a container with slots for each day of the week. I now set up every medicine that Nate takes regularly, which makes it easy for him to take personal responsibility for taking his medicine. At a young age, he knows exactly what slot he should take his medication from at any time of the day. There is never any confusion, because anyone can look at the slots and see if the medicines are still there or if Nate has taken them. Any time I have prescription medicines for myself or any of my family members, I set them up this way. All little lessons of life matter to me.

The Scriptures put emphasis on God's people's acquiring knowledge. Many times, I have made poor choices because I did not take time to understand what my choices would cost me. God's principles remain, however. I miss out on many of His blessings because I don't take time to understand His Word and how He works. It have found it helpful to invest time in understanding His Word so that I am able to pray with more confidence when it comes to the situations I face. I also realize that education is continuous. I will have to keep learning and growing until the day I leave this earth. I have committed to doing this, because it helps.

Discernment Is Awesome

Have you ever entered a home and right away felt that something was different, only to find out later there had been a fight before you arrived? Have you ever met someone and felt great about that person only to find out that he or she was a wonderful person? Have you ever been in a house and sensed that something was not right, only to find out later that the house caught on fire after you left? All these things are signs of God's Spirit in our hearts. Discernment reveals to you exactly what is happening before it is made clear to most people around you.

Discernment in Christian contexts is perception in the absence of judgment, which helps a person obtain spiritual direction and understanding. It is the ability to understand spiritual truth. According to the Bible, we are required to test all things. "But test everything; hold fast what is good. Abstain from every form of evil" (1 Thessalonians 5:21–22 ESV). "Beloved, do not believe every spirit, but test the spirits to see whether they are from God, for many false prophets have gone out into the world" (1 John 4:1 ESV). The ability to test things and to see them from God's point of view is what is known as discernment. Discernment, as mentioned above, gives you the ability to see accurately what is not evident to many people around you.

Spiritual discernment is not meant only for some people; it is available to all believers. Since you cannot have wisdom if you don't have discernment, discernment is to be desired by all believers. No one can have spiritual discernment without God. It has been part of my practice to ask God for discernment about situations, people, environments, etc. As much as I have had trouble in my life, praying for discernment has saved me a lot more trouble. The more I pay attention to my spirit, the more I tend to move forward unhindered.

During my work as a spiritual care provider, I found myself changing my schedule many times, because I felt a confidence in my spirit to do so. I went to see people I had not planned on seeing that day only to find that the person was dying, or only to find out later that the person died after I left. Sometimes I have been in a home where I sensed things in my spirit, so I started to pray in my heart about finding a leading for what else to pray for and what to do. Often when people are dying, they experience a lot of anxiety about death. Death is something none of us has been through; it must difficult to wait for something you have never experienced. When I entered some of these environments, I felt overwhelmed in my spirit right away. My natural person was saying, "Leave. Get out of here." Of course I never left. What I did was intentionally bring a calm to the environment by staying calm in prayer for the person I was visiting. Many times, I let the person take my hand. At first I felt like I was electrocuted with anxiety. But as I resisted anxiety in my spirit and prayed for the person, I noticed that the person started to calm down. Eventually I felt comfortable in the person's presence because he or she had become calm.

In my personal life, I have known confidently in my heart things that other people thought me crazy to believe, only for them to see the proof of it later. Discernment keeps me peaceful. It also helps me know whom to be around and at what times. Not everyone is meant to be around us throughout our entire lives. Some people are meant to be in our lives only for a season; others, for a reason; and others, for a lifetime. It is important to know the difference. People can be very good for you, but having a good person in your life at the wrong time can turn out to be a bad thing. Praying for discernment helps us in all situations when we are consistent with listening to and then following the leading.

I Have Had to Encourage Myself

"Be strong and take heart, all you who hope in the Lord" (Psalm 31:24).

There comes a time in life when you realize that life is busy and that the people in your life have their own lives. They have their problems and their joys. Sometimes your sorrows get in the way of the people whom you love and who love you. I have not been able to be there for many people who needed me. That is life.

While it is wonderful to have people in my life, I have found that there are times when even those who are closest to me can't feel my pain. I know they love me, but the fact is that they don't get it. Other times, for whatever reasons, people are not in a place to support me when I need them most. This is not because they don't care. They may be needing my support at the same time I need their support. Matthew 26:36–56 (ESV) is a great example of this.

> Then Jesus went with them to a place called Gethsemane, and he said to his disciples, "Sit here, while I go over there and pray." And taking with him Peter and the two sons of Zebedee, he began to be sorrowful and troubled. Then he said to them, "My soul is very sorrowful, even to death; remain here, and watch with me." And going a little farther he fell on his face and prayed, saying, "My Father, if it be possible, let this cup pass from me; nevertheless, not as I will, but as you will." And he came to the disciples and found them sleeping. And he said to Peter, "So, could you not watch with me one hour? Watch and pray that you may not enter into temptation. The

spirit indeed is willing, but the flesh is weak." Again, for the second time, he went away and prayed, "My Father, if this cannot pass unless I drink it, your will be done." And again he came and found them sleeping, for their eyes were heavy. So, leaving them again, he went away and prayed for the third time, saying the same words again. Then he came to the disciples and said to them, "Sleep and take your rest later on. See, the hour is at hand, and the Son of Man is betrayed into the hands of sinners. Rise, let us be going; see, my betrayer is at hand."

Sometimes, people have judged me negatively. Thankfully, I see this happen throughout the Bible. First Samuel 30:6 (NKJV) is a good a good example. "And David was greatly distressed; for the people spoke of stoning him, because the soul of all the people was grieved, every man for his sons and for his daughters: but David encouraged himself in the Lord his God." People are entitled to their opinion. The only thing I have found to do in a situation where people are judging me is to pick myself up and crawl to my God. He will never leave me or forsake me. When no one else can feel me, He feels me; when no one else understands, He does.

Forgiving Is Necessary

Witnessing what forgiving myself and others did for me was one of the most freeing lessons of my life. Holding onto un forgiveness holds us captive when we think we are hurting the other person. Understanding God's grace has brought a lot of peace to my heart. What the Lord taught me is that receiving wholeheartedly is a sign of humility. Many people don't know how to receive without feeling that they should do something to pay back. God wants us to receive His gift of grace like our little children receive gifts from us parents. Understanding this helped me learn to forgive myself. I don't have to do anything more; He did it all for me. Likewise, I find peace in forgiving and releasing others, primarily because this is a command from God. In Matthew 6:14–15 (NASB), Jesus says, "For if you forgive others for their transgressions, your heavenly Father will also forgive you. But if you do not forgive others, then your Father will not forgive your transgressions." Whatever God commands us to do is always for our own good. What helps me to practice forgiveness is to understand what forgiveness is not. The fact is that every time I have made a choice to forgive someone for something, I have felt better than if I had held onto my resentment. It takes a lot of energy to hold onto un forgiveness. Forgiving people helps me to relate to others. It also keeps God's blessings flowing in my life.

Being Okay with Personal Boundaries

A boundary is a mark that shows an area's outermost limits. I believe in having boundaries to mark my limits. Personal boundaries are guidelines that I come up with to keep myself safe. I put a limit on how others may behave toward me. Boundaries are usually built out of spiritual beliefs, cultural beliefs, past experiences, people's opinions, and the like. Since life is not fair and since not everyone thinks as I do or wants what I want, I find it necessary to set limits for myself. Thankfully, I have not struggled much with setting boundaries. For this, I give credit to my parents. I believe that having boundaries helps me to relate better to those around me. It also helps me have an awareness of other people's boundaries.

I am okay with saying no, because I am not able to say yes to everything. For example, in the area of giving, most everywhere I turn I am asked to give for this good cause or for that good cause. I am a giver by nature, so I had to learn how to set a boundary in this area by praying and making a decision ahead of time about whom I will give to, why, how much, and how often.

My example of a person who had strong boundaries is Jesus. He loved everyone completely, but He selected only twelve people to be His apostles. Out of those twelve, He was closest to three. And out of those three, one was closest to Him. Boundaries not only keep me safe; they also keep those I love safe. Take my children for example. I maintain my boundaries with them. I am their mom and they are my children, and we cannot be equal in the relationship. I don't need them to like me or to be happy with me all the time. I want them to be good so that in the future they will be good citizens of their country. I teach them to build their own boundaries as well.

My parents raised me and my siblings with strong boundaries. The schools I went to reemphasized the importance of having boundaries. That was helpful for me as an adult in setting boundaries for myself, even though I did not have a full understanding of what that meant. When I started studying divinity in college, I learned more about boundaries and why it is important to have them. As a limited human being, I have found that boundaries are necessary.

Family, and Other Important Relationships

Having people around me who truly care for me as a person has helped me to cope with life. I don't believe that any person is able to get through life alone. From my family to my friends, and including doctors, coworkers, church mates, teachers, et al., I have been blessed with people who have provided me with a lot of support.

Although I may not be able to express my gratitude to each person in a way that matters to them specifically, I am aware that I would not have made it this far without each and every one of them. I hold dearly very many people. I smile a lot when thinking of moments I've shared with others. I think of the sacrifices my parents have made for me throughout my life, the strong bond of love and support from all of my siblings, the commitment from many of my friends. I recall the multiple baby showers put together for both of my children by my friends so that my children did not lack. I remember a time when my Kenyan friends who live in the Minneapolis area came together and raised money to support me one of the times my son was hospitalized for a long period of time. I remember my friend Jennifer carrying three of her babies to the hospital to see Nathanael and me several times. That meant a lot to me, as did the support of many other friends who sacrificed so much for me. I am grateful for my boss's understanding and support, and for my coworkers' sacrifices, including when they came to sit with me in my very messy apartment when I was sick and needed them. I am thankful for the many friends who faithfully came to the hospital when Nate was an inpatient. Here I mention only some people who helped out. The list is longer, but I am not able to thank everyone specifically. Many people have been there for me during extremely vulnerable times of my life. There is no way for me to thank them enough. I simply am left in awe. I pray for these people when I think of how they have been there for me. I will forever hold in my heart some people who are not aware of how dearly I hold them.

Moments of Solitude

As wonderful as it is to have people around me who love me, I find that it is in my moments of solitude when God did His inner work in me. I seek moments of solitude in my life regularly, because I realize it does my heart a lot of good. Those are the moments when I can bring my heart naked before God. Those are the moments when I get spiritual surgery and healing. Those are the moments when my heart calms down from experiencing life's chaos.

Solitude gives me a place to do a self-evaluation on my true emotions, my thought life, and other things of importance to me (like my children). When I am alone, I count my blessings and remain in gratitude. Being alone gives me a chance to pay attention to how my body is feeling so I can determine if I need to do something about it. For example, when I get my mind on something, I easily become too busy and deprive myself of sleep. Intentional moments of solitude force me to pay attention to how my business is affecting my health and my eating patterns, and why. That helps me to deal with most problems sooner rather than later.

Moments of solitude also give me a comfortable time to do some of the things that are not comfortable to do with other people around, for example, making out loud confessions to counter negative thoughts or emotions, crying if need be without being asked why I am crying, or just being.

Exercise, Nutrition, and General Health

It takes discipline to live a healthy life. Practicing discipline leads to a healthy lifestyle. Working in health care systems has taught me many things, one of which is that I shouldn't do too many things at once, as this will have a negative effect on my health. It takes time to see results of the things I do to improve my health. I am aware that some conditions are beyond people's control, but most of what affects most people are things that can be controlled or made better if one has the intention to do so.

The moment I made up my mind to start exercising regularly, I started to exercise. It then became something I needed to do. There are times I get out of the habit for one reason or another. During those times, my body knows that it is lacking something. Exercise helps me sleep better at night, helps my body systems work better, helps me feel more calm, and lessens my stress during stressful times. I find that it truly helps me feel better about myself overall.

I pay attention to the food I bring into my home. I don't normally buy chips, cookies, and the like. Those things taste good and are hard to resist, but they are not what my body needs to stay healthy. My children eat all types of vegetables and don't complain about eating them. I eat veggies with my meals, so it is the norm in our home. We eat fruit for a snack. I challenge people, saying that it is possible to give up junk food. If they can buy soda pop, they can buy an orange instead. It does not cost more to eat healthier; it takes intention. For example, why buy diet pop when water flows out of your tap and when drinking water leaves you feeling better than drinking pop? I have been involved with many people who have regretted what they had put into their body only when it was too late to repair the damage caused by eating poorly. You and I don't have to wait until it is too late.

Church Attendance

Gathering with other people in worship is something I believe in and enjoy doing. There is something beautiful about a group of people coming together in the name of God. I don't need to know anyone in the church to enjoy the service. I just need to be around people in worship. I have a church I call my home church, because I like the teachings of inspiration that my pastor is gifted in delivering. I also love our praise and worship team and their ability to usher in the presence of God. When I am among people and singing with them, it brings a sense of wholesomeness to my heart. I can only imagine God smiling as He watches His people gathering together before Him. Being a part of such a gathering blesses my heart. When I miss a church service, I feel it. I feel a sense of emotional rest when I set all the cares of my life aside and live carefree for a two-hour church service. My children have found a safe place in our church. They love to go there, because they feel loved and cared for by those who work in the children's ministry. When we are not at home and cannot attend our home church, we make an effort to find a church we can attend so we can be around other believers. It is refreshing for me to be around other Christians, even when I don't know any of them in particular.

Church provides me with a place to connect with people who end up being a blessing to my life. When I was still very new here in the United States, I met my friend Mary at church. She really blessed my life in those days. Mary supported me when I was pregnant with my son, and she continues to be a blessing to my family today. I met Mac and Joan at church, and they are now the godparents of both of my children. It is a blessing that they take this role seriously. They supported me through both of my pregnancies. Joan was present like a mom would be when both of my children were born, each under tough circumstances. She awoke very early on different occasions to be at the hospital with me when my son was having surgery. In addition, Mac and Joan adopted me into their family, since my family live so far away. My pastors have also supported me at various times along my journey. I have also had other relationships that developed because I belonged to a church. Church has definitely strengthened my spiritual life, and I am thankful for that.

Journaling

Journaling is one of the ways I get things out of my mind, especially if it is something I am trying not to forget. I write down my thoughts, my feelings, and the events of my life. Once I have whatever it is written down, I find that my mind relaxes. I don't have to hang onto the matter any longer. I can always go and read about it if I need to. That really helps me.

Journaling has helped me with writing this book. Without my journals, it would not have been possible for me to sit down and, within a month or two, come up with this book. I love writing. I have many writing projects in the works. I used to have many papers strewn all over. I am thankful for computers and I Pads, as I don't lose them as I used to lose papers and books.

Another reason I journal is in order to keep the facts as facts. It is one thing to try to recall what happened in a certain situation and another thing to know for a fact what happened, because you have it written down as it happened then. I have found facts to be helpful on many occasions. When they haven't been helpful, I know I have done my best in providing what I know.

I Made a Decision Never to Quit

"Life is tough, and only the tough make it" is a statement I heard all my life growing up, although I didn't quite understand it until much later in my life. It is understandable that some individuals end up with life conditions that limit them in terms of what they can achieve. Yet even some of the limited people do much better in life than many who have fewer limitations. I believe success is measured by each person's purpose. We cannot compare ourselves to others in order to determine who is the more successful. However, each person knows deep inside when he or she has succeeded. I have never had much money, but I have felt very successful in being a mother to my children. I have had other successes along the way. I fight for my life. I don't worry about what those around me have or where they are in life. I just want to fulfill my assignment here on earth. That is my goal.

When God blessed me with Nathanael, I felt that life was very tough. Sometimes I was so overwhelmed that I did not know what to do. Many times I felt like I was going to melt away under the pressures of life. It was during this season of my life when I looked at myself in the mirror and realized that I needed to make a profound decision concerning my life before I let circumstances make that decision for me. I had started feeling that I did not matter anymore and that I was not necessary in life, but I had a child who, I knew deep within my heart, needed his mother. I can't tell you that I know what decision I would have made at that time were it not for my son. But I know one thing: my son was the reason I made the decision not to quit. That decision led to my ability to face life and to do what I needed to do for my son. Later on, I thanked God for that decision—and I made it again for myself the next time. I decided to fight for my life no matter what it brought. I decided to fight for my children and for my purpose in life. That decision has brought me a long way in light of the many things that followed. Making the decision ahead of time helped when tough times came.

I Choose to Work Hard

Proverbs 10:4 (ESV): "A slack hand causes poverty, but the hand of the diligent makes rich."

One of my favorite things to do is to sleep. Many people who know me would have a hard time believing this about me, because it is not what they see. When my head lands on my pillow, I go out. I sleep very well too, unless something is going on with my children and I intend to check on them throughout the night. It is a great feeling just to lie in bed in the morning and not be in a hurry. It is very rare that I have a disturbed night when I can't sleep. I am very thankful for that.

Knowing this fact about myself made it necessary for me to make the decision to work hard for my life and for my children's sake. I don't like being awake in the middle of the night when everyone else is sleeping, but that is what I have to do to fulfill my calling. I trained myself to make decisions after enumerating my reason for each decision. Working with people during their end of life reinforced my decision-making processes. Many people, when dying, reflect on the things they wish they had done. Being exposed to this regularly made me think about my own life and what I can do to avoid having regrets. It is the reason I am happy to be awake at two in the morning, working instead of sleeping soundly, the latter of which is what I would prefer to do. Providing end-of-care support brought me to the realization that life on earth is not forever and is not as long as we may like to believe it is. A hundred years of life is not that long. Working hard is how I managed to keep a job for ten years under tough circumstances. As much as my employer cared for me, there was still work to be done. If I did not do it, then I am sure my employer would have found someone else to do it. Knowing this made me work without complaining, no matter where I did my work from or what my personal circumstances were. I did not want to lose my job, so I put forth effort to keep it.

Another major reason I choose to work hard is because I want to raise my children a certain way. I also have a lot I want to give to other people. I want to spend a lot of time with my children, and I would like to be a blessing to other people. That leaves me needing more time in a day. I have to make a choice and do my best to stay focused. I hardly watch TV. Most of the time, I do the things that I have in my mind to do. I have found that I don't have much idle time. This is not to say that I don't have fun in life. I play with my children and do fun things with them, knowing I am doing it for their sake and not because I have nothing else to do. I spend time with my husband intentionally for the purpose of growing our relationship. Other than being intentional about people in my life, I embrace work, because it helps me get what I want for my children and for myself.

One day when I was a single mother, I was totally broke, so I decided to go to a place where, I was told, food and diapers were handed out. I could not find food to eat, as the place offered only foods I was not used to. I did not know what most of the food was. I got some diapers though, and I brought them home. I was thankful. I know that someone had given those diapers with love. While the diapers helped me for a few days, I found that they leaked. I did not like the fact that they were leaking even though they were helpful. I did not like the fact that I could not find help with food even though there was food available. I prefer to go to the store and buy exactly what I choose, but I could not do this without money. These are some of the reasons I choose to work instead of to sleep at night.

One of the things my mother taught all of her girls was never to live our lives expecting to get married to a man who would take care of our needs. My mother had an excellent husband, my dad, who was a great provider for his family and who really cared for all of us. In spite of this, my mother said there were times when she really wanted something that my dad thought was unnecessary. She taught by example that, most times, men do not enjoy spending money. There were many things my dad thought were unnecessary, but he turned out to be the first one to thoroughly enjoy that thing once it was in our home. My mother taught us that a woman's being self-reliant makes her relationship with her husband better. Being able to go and get some of what she really wanted without asking for everything from her husband kept my mother less stressed out. It became pretty evident to me at an early age that no matter how good a man I married, he would not satisfy my desires. My dad was a such a great husband to my mom, but he did not agree with everything she wanted for herself or for us, their kids. My mom was extravagant; she wanted nice things. My dad did not think it was necessary for her to buy something new if she already had an old one. He would wear a shirt until the collar fell off if you let him—as long as it was clean. My parents did not fight over what Mom wanted, because she was a trouper of a woman and was not afraid to work hard. She would tell us things like, "When you don't get what you want, don't waste your energy and time being upset about it. Instead, use your energy and time to do something about it." As a result of Mom's example, all of her daughters are very hard workers and are self-reliant. I make it a goal, when I want to get something for my kids, for my husband, or for myself, to work for it and get it. When I can't afford it, I don't expect it from anyone. If someone else gets it for me, I am very thankful, because it was not expected. That keeps me peaceful, thanks to my mommy.

I Choose to Honor My Parents, to Treat Them with Respect

"Honor your father and your mother, that your days may be long in the land that the Lord your God is giving you" (Exodus 20:12 ESV).

Last but not least of the things I would like to mention in this section is having respect for parents and the elderly. When my parents were raising us children, they were not shy about teaching us the benefit of obeying the commandment to honor one's parents. They did not emphasize it simply because they were selfish or wanted to control us. They did it because they wanted us to be blessed. They did not just leave the matter after teaching it to us; they made sure we practiced the commandment. Showing disrespect to our parents or to older people was not an option for us children. We were raised with love and discipline; one did not exist without the other. I did not always agree with my parents, but I knew very well they were the parents and I wasn't. Not one of us children dared talk back to my parents. It was as simple as that.

I grew up watching how my parents treated their own parents. It was the very same way, with respect. My dad's mom died before I was born, but I grew up with all my other grandparents. I watched my grandfather be unreasonable with my mom or my dad, neither of whom acted in a disrespectful way toward him. They never replied to him in anger. They took care of their parents to the very end and did not get tired of it. They expected us children to help take care of our grandparents, and we did. It was very special when my grandfather would spit on our hands as a sign of blessing us. Yes, I mean spit. We loved doing things for him so that he could spit on us to bless us. I also watched my mom take care of other older people in the village, as she took me with her many times. She often talked about what a blessing it would eventually be for me when I did the same once I was an adult.

As an adult, I think it is still very important to treat my parents well. I love them and want them to know that I appreciate the sacrifices they made for me. I love to talk to my parents and listen to them tell me how much they pray for me and my siblings. I love to hear them speak blessings over my life. It means the world to me and has helped me in spite of the distance between us. I also love to be a blessing to the elderly people around me, especially my husband's mother. I believe this does something for my life. As my mother liked to emphasize, the fifth commandment is the only commandment with promise attached to it.

Part Five

Spiritual Care for God's People

The Harvest Is Plentiful; the Laborers, Few

> And Jesus went throughout all the cities and villages, teaching in their synagogues and proclaiming the gospel of the kingdom and healing every disease and every affliction. When he saw the crowds, he had compassion for them, because they were harassed and helpless, like sheep without a shepherd. Then he said to his disciples, "The harvest is plentiful, but the laborers are few; therefore pray earnestly to the Lord of the harvest to send out laborers into his harvest." (Matthew 9:35–38 ESV)

My Call to Ministry

Becoming a hospice chaplain was not something I had dreamt of. Even though I always knew that I had a heart for people who were suffering and in pain, I never imagined that I would become submerged in that kind of ministry. I started off by attempting to become a Catholic nun at sixteen years of age. My dad did not think I was old enough to make that decision, so he discouraged me, for which I am glad. I cannot imagine my life without my children. At the same time, however, I have a lot of respect for any person who commits his or her entire life to the ministry, forsaking family life. At the age of eighteen, I made a personal decision to accept Christ. That was when I realized that my going to church or having been born in a Christian family did not automatically make me a Christian. I needed to make my own choice to become a Christian, because faith is not a family deal but a personal choice. I did not have much knowledge of the Bible other than

177

what was taught to me at church while I was growing up. I started feeling that I needed to understand more of the Bible for myself. When I relocated to the United States, I tried different colleges, and different careers that worked directly with people. I tried hospitality careers and nursing, but my heart did not sit with any of them. As I continued my search to understand the Word of God and what being involved in ministry meant, I enrolled in a Bible college. That was the first time I felt in my heart that I was in the right place and doing the right thing. That was one of the happiest times of my adult life. I started getting involved in ministry and was invited to fellowships and to some churches to preach. I also supported individuals. Eventually, once I finished my BA in divinity, I was ordained as a minister.

As time went by, I envisioned starting an organization to build homes for orphans and abandoned children in Kenya. I also dreamt of writing books on the topics about which I felt passionate. Little did I know that the visions that seemed easiest and closest weren't going to materialize for many years.

Once I had my son, all my dreams went into hibernation. I began living for the moment. My dreams remained in my heart. I prayed about them every day during my season in the valley. I had peace in knowing that what God has begun, He will bring to accomplishment. I did not feel any need to struggle and try to bring anything to pass. I knew if these things were God's will for my life, then it was a matter of time before they materialized. I set it in my heart to walk with Him one day at a time, taking care of what needed my attention—and that was my son. In the process, God opened other doors to see me through the season. In His faithfulness, He opened the door for me to become a spiritual care provider. God made me a full-time minister when I least expected it to happen in my life. At the age of thirty-two, going through a divorce and dealing with my son's medical problems, I became a hospice chaplain. It was extremely humbling to be in that position. It worked well for me, because I have a heart for people when they are hurting. Working with thousands of people facing death, getting to know many of them, and watching them die gave me such a respect for life. Working with grieving caregivers and family was exactly what I needed to get through my own tough journey, because I didn't feel that I was alone in suffering anymore. Working for a period of ten years, I ministered to people who were going through grief and loss. This work didn't take away the pain of my own life; instead, it gave me a different lens through which to view my life, which really helped me. I was always reminded that I was not grieving, which kept me very thankful to God in my process. Moreover, I am thankful to God because He knows what I need for each season of my life before I realize my own need. I can acknowledge that He is so good at working out the details of my life when I depend on Him. Paying attention to His voice and trusting His voice is key.

As a Hospice Chaplain

Working as a hospice chaplain gave me a lot of exposure to death and dying, grief, churches, and, more than everything else, people's brokenness as well as their spiritual and emotional needs. I had the honor of listening to many stories about people's experiences in life, as fathers, mothers, veterans, children, friends, husbands, wives, etc. I grew a lot, and very fast, thanks to the nature of my work. I learned to embrace death as part of life, and I found peace for myself through my faith in Jesus Christ. The reality of how fast life can change hit home for me. I met many people who had been living their lives as usual only to hear from a doctor that they would die within a week. I watched this happen many times. Some people would be in the process of sharing their story with me, but when I came back the next day or in two days, they were not able to talk at all. I watched death happen in a matter of days, just like the doctor had predicted. It was very eye-opening for me. It is possible to meet a person who looks healthy and alive and then to attend his or her funeral in a week's time. It happens regularly. The frightening thing is that it could happen to anyone.

Listening to people's stories was such a blessing to me. Working with veterans and hearing their stories filled my heart with gratitude for all those who sacrificed their lives for the people of their country. It is a huge sacrifice. I was very honored to learn as many things as I did about veterans. During wartime, many veterans go through horrific experiences. During deployment, they are separated from their families. I worked with people who had bullet scars. They shared their stories of what they went through during that season of their lives and how that changed them. Many of them watched their friends be killed right before their eyes. Others had to kill people and then live with that knowledge. Many of them lived with a lot of guilt. Many of them found it difficult to fit in with their families after coming back from war. One of the majors complaints I heard from veterans was that people did not understand them when they came back from serving. Many of them went through their lives feeling unheard.

I worked with people who were dying of illnesses. It is very difficult to wait for death day in and day out. It is hard to tell whether it would be better to die instantly of a car accident or to be told you are dying of cancer in a month or in six months. I met a few people who just took it easy and said that every day they'd had since learning of their prognosis was a gift. I learned a lot from these people as well. Those who tended to take it easy lived longer than expected and were more peaceful as they waited to die. This type of person didn't come without challenges though, because illness affects not just one person but the whole family.

Another aspect of my work involved working with the caregivers, who were more often than not related to the patient. Providing support for and facilitating some discussions between family members was always an honor for me. For example, I helped planned funerals, helped people discuss their wishes, and helped mend rifts when it was difficult for a person to express his or her true feelings. Watching many caregivers spend sleepless nights was such an encouragement to me, although those people did not know that. I believe I supported these caregivers well, because I felt for them in ways that school did not teach me to feel. It was always sad to see caregivers say good-bye to their loved ones. Many times I conducted bedside services to facilitate the process of the family's saying good-bye and stating anything that was important for them to say before their loved one died. I, coming from a culture that does not talk about death or accept it, experienced a great deal of growth. My prayer is that when it comes time for my parents to die I may be there to sit beside them and hold their hand like I did for many other people.

I have brought up the topics of death and last wishes with my family. It was not easy to do, but I did it because I do not want any of my family, including me, to die alone if I can help it. In my culture, people live as if no one will ever die. When someone is dying, most people tend to disappear from that person's life. I wish I would see more people being involved with and supporting their loved ones, knowing that we are all going to walk through the gate of death someday. I have witnessed the sense of peace and closure that comes when people can come together and talk about faith and their hope of meeting again. I have seen dying people experience peace when their loved ones are around them. On the other hand, some people like to be left alone when they are dying. Somehow they let others know this, even though they can't talk. It is amazing how spiritual we are and how spiritually we are connected to each other. Working with families was hard for me because I had to say good-bye to them too after their loved ones died. Many times I wondered how the families fared in the aftermath.

Officiating funerals and memorial services, as well as doing baptisms, was something I did as well. I was very honored to play such a role for dying people and their families. It surprised me how many funerals and memorial services I conducted as a chaplain. I could not begin to count how many I did in my ten years with Hospice of the Twin Cities. What surprised me was the realization of how many people do not belong to a church congregation although they are Christians. Many people had their reasons for this, reasons that were sad for me to hear. Before I became a chaplain, I thought that people normally held the aforementioned types of ceremonies at churches, but a lot of people are members of no church when they die. That fact was disturbing to my mind. I was left wondering if churches are aware of this fact.

God's People

People around us are searching for the meaning of their existence. As humans, we want to know who we are and why we are here. Most people want to help and to receive help more than anything else. In other words, they are seeking a faith they can trust. Working as a chaplain was always a blessing for me because I got to work with people. It also brought sadness to my heart, especially when I realized how many people were without a pastor or a church. Many of the people to whom I ministered had been church members but had left their church for various reasons. People like this are out there, seeking a place they can call home. Many other people have been led into other, non-Christian beliefs because they found themselves cared for by people of other religions. In my ten years at Hospice of the Twin Cities, I worked with thousands of patients and their families. Of these people, a large percentage were Christians who did not belong to a church. Most of them had a sad story to tell about what had happened that had caused them to decide to leave their church. One of the stories I heard was as follows: "When my wife was dying, I called my church, but no one from my church came to visit during that season. I figured I may as well not belong to a church." Other people said when they got too sick to go to church, people from their church visited for a while but then stopped visiting. There were very many stories told by people who felt that their church did not show them care when they were in need. Although money issues and interpersonal conflicts were mentioned as reasons for why people had left the church, the greatest thing mentioned was neglect during a person's time of need. I also heard stories of many people who called a church for help and were told, simply and clearly, "You do not belong to this church. Sorry." As a result, these people went on to adopt different religions, ones where they found people who cared more. I was a pastor for many, anointing people with oil, providing Communion service, etc. This showed me that people are very hungry for God and truth even if they have lost trust in the community of their church. I wonder what Christ would have done in these situations.

I also met people who did not want to belong to a church because they didn't believe in belonging to a church. Still, I don't believe that those who don't want to belong to a church should be ignored by the church—but I see this as a separate issue. Every person is, to a great extent, responsible for his or her own faith and beliefs. I am left wondering if church members stay within their church building and wait for broken people to come looking for a church. Should church members go out to look for broken people and then bring them to church? I wonder if churches have set aside in their budgets money specifically dedicated to caring for people in the church or for people in the community at large. I wonder if church-related programs have become more important to churches than the members of the congregations are. It also seems that churches are waiting for people to need to belong to the church. In the meantime, people who are seeking a church end up joining a religion, Christian or not, whose followers show that they care.

I don't have answers. I am left with a lot of questions. I have never worked in any church setting, but based on the stories I listened to day after day from churchless Christians, I have my reasons for believing that the Church of Christ in general has lost sight of the Great Commission that was left by our Lord.

I Wonder

"When he saw the crowds, he had compassion for them, because they were harassed and helpless, like sheep without a shepherd. Then he said to his disciples, 'The harvest is plentiful, but the laborers are few; therefore pray earnestly to the Lord of the harvest to send out laborers into his harvest.'"

What I see in Jesus is compassion for people who are broken. I wonder how much compassion is left in the Church of Christ. Are churches today operating as a club operates? Even among the members, do churches seem to cater more to those who put more money in the offering basket? Do churches answer the calls of richer members differently than they answer the calls of those who have less to offer? Are churches really telling people who call in need that they can't help them because they don't belong to the church? Are pastors expecting too much from people and forgetting that the same people are broken and in need? Could it be that churches are not increasing in number because people aren't cared for by the church when they are in need? According to Acts 4:32–35, every person who was a believer was cared for by other believers. People brought what they had to the apostles, and the apostles made sure the believers were taken care of. They did not ignore the current believers in the church and use all their resources to preach to those who were not part of the church. They ministered to all alike. They took care of believers, and they reached out to those who were not believers and brought them in. Yet I heard numerous stories from believers who were neglected by their churches when they had nothing to give to the church. What would happen if churches put people first, as was done in the early church?

Could it be that people don't give as much of their money to their church because they don't trust their church to be there for them in their time of need? How about the presence of the church in people's lives during times of need? How many believers call a church when they are in need, only to be told, "We will put you on our prayer list"? The people I listened to did not feel cared for simply because their church put them on a prayer list, notwithstanding how important prayer is. These people needed their pastors or fellow church members to come and sit with them for an hour or so just to show they cared. I personally was very impressed by the Catholic church my mother attended while she was in the United States for a year and half to help me with my son.

My mother ended up having hip replacement surgery and could not go to church for a while. People of that church, even though my mom was only temporarily fellowshipping with them, came to see her at home once every week, just to sit with her and provide her with Holy Communion. It was amazing to see what that did for my mom. Even today, my mother holds that church deeply in her heart. But such was not the story I heard from the people to whom I ministered who belonged to no church, which was sad. Many said they watched their loved ones die without anyone from their church ever showing up or else after someone showed up just once.

Being that every person, including every believer, is broken, is there any way that churches can set their budgets so that the believers within the congregation are cared for better, not so much by giving money but by being present for their fellows in the latter's times of need? How about having ministries whose members extend their arms to callers who are not members of that church? How about having a team that can meet a person somewhere safe and lend a listening ear, if nothing else? Might such a gesture lead a person to believe in Christ and to attend that very church or another church someday? It is true the harvest is plentiful. Are churches focused on developing more leaders to help care for believers within the church instead of reaching out to those outside the church? In Exodus 18:15–23, Moses receives this advice from his father-in-law, who was a priest:

> And Moses said to his father-in-law, "Because the people come to me to inquire of God. When they have a difficulty, they come to me, and I judge between one and another; and I make known the statutes of God and His laws." So Moses' father-in-law said to him, "The thing that you do is not good. Both you

and these people who are with you will surely wear yourselves out. For this thing is too much for you; you are not able to perform it by yourself. Listen now to my voice; I will give you counsel, and God will be with you: Stand before God for the people, so that you may bring the difficulties to God. And you shall teach them the statutes and the laws, and show them the way in which they must walk and the work they must do. Moreover you shall select from all the people able men, such as fear God, men of truth, hating covetousness; and place such over them to be rulers of thousands, rulers of hundreds, rulers of fifties, and rulers of tens. And let them judge the people at all times. Then it will be that every great matter they shall bring to you, but every small matter they themselves shall judge. So it will be easier for you, for they will bear the burden with you. If you do this thing, and God so commands you, then you will be able to endure, and all this people will also go to their place in peace."

I wonder: if the churches raised more leaders, would this lead more believers to stay in the church and lead more people to come into that church—instead of people going to seek help elsewhere? Since believers do give money to the church they attend, I wonder what difference it would make if this money were used to help the people who give regularly instead of expecting those people to give their money and then to go for help elsewhere in their times of need. From the stories I have listened to, I determined that most people are not looking for much. People just want to know that they matter and are cared for.

Part Six

My Family of Origin

Helping children develop a strong backbone is important, because you never know what they will encounter in their lives. I believe that how my parents raised me has played a very big role in helping me fight hard for my life. They strengthened my spirit regularly by building me up and being present for me always. We children knew that we were our parents' priority. My parents were both calm people with a strong outlook to life. One of the things I am very thankful for is that they did not spoon-feed us. They did not make it seem as if we didn't need to work. If anything, my dad was good at reminding us that all he could give us was an education. He said that after that we would be on our own. He reminded us that his home belonged to him and his wife, and that we children were to live there for a short time only. My parents gave me and my siblings a good life, reminding us that we would be responsible for what we did with our own lives once we graduated college. I believe that this message kept all of us focused. Also, we were not bailed out when our actions brought unwanted consequences. When we messed up, we faced the consequences.

My parents cooperated with each other when they parented us. When one of them said no, you saw no need to ask the other one, because his or her answer would be an obvious no. My mother raised us always to be there for each other as siblings. She never came between her children when there was a disagreement. She always helped us mend things though. She still does this, but with our marriages. She is the type of mother who refuses to talk about a person with whom one of her children is angry. She holds us all accountable, too. That is how she raised us. As siblings, we have remained very close in spite of the physical distance between us. We trust each other and look out for each other. None of us ever demanded anything from our parents. We were trained to be grateful for what we have. After each of us graduated from school, we were prepared to move on—and our parents were prepared to release us. I think they felt they had done a good job of raising us, because they sent us all off with blessings when the time came.

My parents raised us in faith. In addition to going to church every Sunday, we prayed together every morning and every night as a family. My mother prayed about everything. When God answered her prayer, she was sure to declare it before her family. Although my mother was an exceptionally hard worker and a wise woman, she never prided herself on her hard work. Instead, she testified to God's power and provision for everything. When she brought home a basket full of mangoes she had bought, she would say, "I thank God for providing these mangoes for my children." While we were growing up, we teased Mom for always praying, even when she was walking along the road or working in the garden. My parents modeled faith to us and also encouraged us to have our own faith. They talked about how important it was to have God leading our lives on a regular basis. While our parents were raising us, going to church was a must for all of us, whether we wanted to go or not.

Education was another aspect of life that my parents believed in and put emphasis on. Although my parents married very young, they educated themselves and eventually went back to college, earning degrees that led them to get their jobs. My dad's dream was to see his children achieve as much education as they could. He talked to us about how difficult it was for him and my mom to earn their degrees while raising us, saying that they did not quit regardless. Because they worked hard, they were able to provide for us. They also made sacrifices to send us to good schools. I was eleven years old when I was taken to a Catholic boarding school. Although I did not like being in a boarding school, it was a good choice, as it provided a good academic environment, which was very important to my parents. When I was growing up, a good academic background was viewed as the only way to succeed in life. The better a person was academically, the more likely he or she was to find a better job and to live a better life. My parents put everything they could into paying for our education. I will forever be grateful for that.

During our school breaks, my parents, especially my mom, took time off work to be home with us. It was important to her to be around her children. I will never forget how happy and fulfilled she seemed to be when she was around us. My parents were both home in the evenings. They shared many stories of their lives as well as of life in general. They enjoyed being around us, which made our relationships with them very easy throughout our childhood and into our adulthood.

Neither of my parents were raised in a strong family, but they chose to start a strong family of their own. I have met many people who had grown up in hardship and have gone on to do very well in their lives. I learned from my parents and from people like them that I can choose my life. Even as a single mother, I stayed mindful of how I wanted my son to be once he was grown and facing his own life. I have come to believe that faith, family, and education are the basis for a successful human life. I want to give to my children what my parents gave to me.

My Father's Heart

One night, I awoke in the middle of the night and needed to use the bathroom. When I was growing up, we did not have a bathroom inside the house. We had to go outside to use the bathroom, because that was where the outhouse stood. When I needed to go at night, I woke my mother to go with me, because I was afraid to go outside by myself. On this night, I knocked at my parents' door. Mom told me to come in. I opened the door and noticed that my dad was sitting on the bed. The curtains were open, and he was looking through the window. I thought that was strange. The next morning, I asked my mother what Dad was doing sitting up and looking through the window in the middle of the night. What she told me made me realize a very special thing about my father. She said that it was usual for Dad to do that. She said, "He sits on that very spot every night thinking about his children and dreaming of his children's success." I will never forget how that made me feel. It was deep and wide. That image of my father remains clear in my mind today.

On another occasion, a neighbor kid did something to me, but I don't remember what it was. I have intended to ask him if he remembers what happened, but I have not seen him in many years. We were getting close to my home on our walk back from school. That was before I went to boarding school. What I remember clearly was my father's reaction when I, crying, entered the gate to our home. His eyes became larger than I had ever seen them before. I started telling him what had happened. Before I finished speaking, he took off. I have never seen my father run so fast in my entire life. The kid ran away. Later, my father shared with Mom how upset he was at the kid. He did not catch up to the kid, but he did go and speak to the boy's father. I am sure that scared the kid enough to never hurt my feelings again after that day. What touched my heart the most was to see my father drop everything and run fast, all because I was hurt. It made me feel very special and cared for. It made me realize how much I meant to my father. I am blessed to have you, Dad, for my father. I love you, and because of the kind of a father you are, I love to think of God as my Father. You are kind, loving, and caring, a provider and a protector who is always there for me. I am very thankful.

My Mother's Dedication

The Grass Tire

One day, my mom set out on a journey to visit my sisters at school. The school was far away from home, and the roads were rough. When Mom was in the middle of nowhere, she noticed that her tire was punctured. In those days, there were no cell phones. There were no homes around, so my mom had no way of contacting anyone for help. She had to figure out a way to get out of there. She had an idea. She looked around for grass and leaves, struggled by herself to remove the tire from its rim, filled the tire with grass and leaves, and then mounted it back on the rim. She managed to do this herself. You would think that at that point my mother would have turned around and gone back home. No! She was going to see her children. She drove her car slowly and safely, eventually reaching her destination and seeing her children. My younger brother and I, very young at the time, had stayed home with Dad. My dad waited and waited, but Mom did not show up when she was supposed to. Eventually my mom got home—at about two o'clock in the morning—driving her car with a grass tire. She had wanted to see her children and did see them, and that was all that mattered to her.

Most education in Kenya, especially high school and college, takes place in boarding schools. Several middle schools, for children ages eleven to fourteen, provide boarding opportunities for those parents who can afford it and are willing to board their children. My parents, being very keen on education, sent their children to boarding schools from about age eleven to eighteen years old, after which time we boarded at college. Without an education, a person may find it difficult to live an okay life in Kenya. Kenya offers nothing like welfare to help people who have no jobs. My parents wanted to give us children the best opportunity for education available, which is why they sent us to boarding school. Boarding schools were known to provide a better education and better discipline, given the fewer distractions.

My mother missed her children very much when we were at boarding school. She wanted to see us as much as she could, and nothing was going to stop her. My mother, a very strong woman, is such a hero. She got married at the age of sixteen years. Instead of becoming bitter, she turned it around and became better. My father helped her go to college for social work because she had such a heart for people. She was such an inspiration to women in particular, although she helped everyone she could. She wanted women to be strong and to know that they could make it through anything. She was well known for participating in women's movements in Kenya in her day. In the way she lived her life, my mother showed me what sacrificing for those you loved meant. She loved people, and she showed it. She did not just offer prayers for people. When someone needed help, she was in the business of figuring out how to make things better for that person. When we had unexpected visitors during mealtimes, she served the food and went without food herself if there wasn't enough. This did not happen once in a blue moon. It happened often. The older we children got, the more we started watching out for Mother to make sure she was taken care of too. Mama, I am blessed to have you for my mother. You taught me enough about strength to last me for my entire lifetime. I love you, Mama.

To both of my parents, know that I, Lucy, Mary, Koome, and Isabella love you and are very grateful for your unconditional love and support throughout every stage of our lives. Our lives would not have been the same without your great wisdom in how you raised us and without the support you continue to give us and our families. My prayer is that God may bless you and sustain you all the days of your life.

My Gratitude

Psalm 29

A Psalm of David

Give unto the Lord, O you mighty ones,
Give unto the Lord glory and strength.
Give unto the Lord the glory due to His name;
Worship the Lord in the beauty of holiness.
The voice of the Lord is over the waters;
The God of glory thunders;
The Lord is over many waters.
The voice of the Lord is powerful;
The voice of the Lord is full of majesty.
The voice of the Lord breaks the cedars,
Yes, the Lord splinters the cedars of Lebanon.
He makes them also skip like a calf,
Lebanon and Sirion like a young wild ox.
The voice of the Lord divides the flames of fire.
The voice of the Lord shakes the wilderness;
The Lord shakes the Wilderness of Kadesh.
The voice of the Lord makes the deer give birth,
And strips the forests bare;
And in His temple everyone says, "Glory!"
The Lord sat enthroned at the Flood,
And the Lord sits as King forever.
The Lord will give strength to His people;
The Lord will bless His people with peace.

My favorite animal is the giraffe.

About the Author

Ann Makena's top priority is raising her children. Her passion is in writing, inspiring others, especially during tough times, as well as the wellbeing of orphans and abandoned children among others. Her heart goes out to oppressed women and single mothers of the world. Ann is a founded a charitable organization that is aimed at building homes for orphans with hopes to change the culture of orphans and abandoned children in Kenya. She is an ordained minister. Ann Makena has a M.A. of Theological studies, B/S in Psychology- counseling, B.A in Divinity. Previously Ann served for 10 years as a full time chaplain for Hospice of the Twin Cities and is currently completing a second M.A. program. She is pursuing M.A. in Ministry leadership.

Printed in the United States
By Bookmasters